THE FABULOUS STORY OF JOHN, PAUL, GEORGE AND RINGO

THE Beatles

OCTOPUS
in association with
Phoebus

CONTENTS

Editorial Consultant Jeremy Pascall / Material Compiled by Robert Burt

ACKNOWLEDGEMENTS
Jacket and prelim pictures are from the following sources:
Camera Press, Mike Cook, L.F.I., Jo Stephens, Syndication
International.

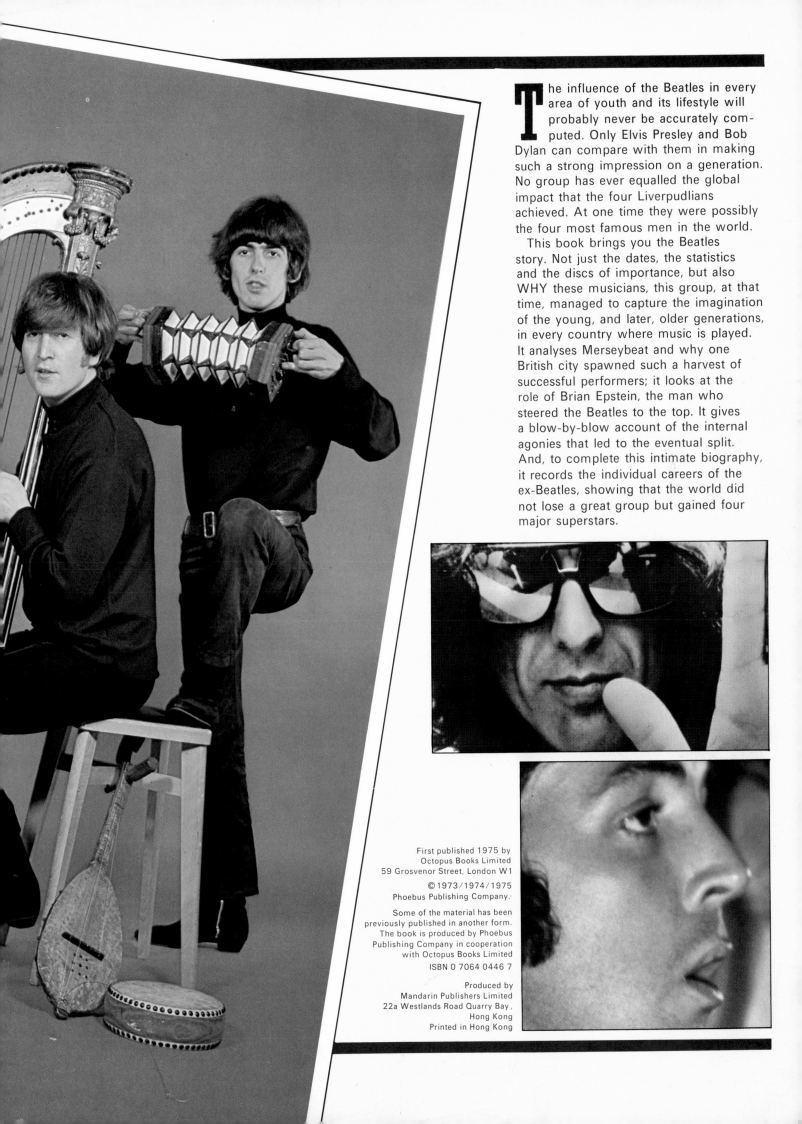

The influence of the Beatles in every area of youth and its lifestyle will probably never be accurately computed. Only Elvis Presley and Bob Dylan can compare with them in making such a strong impression on a generation. No group has ever equalled the global impact that the four Liverpudlians achieved. At one time they were possibly the four most famous men in the world.

This book brings you the Beatles story. Not just the dates, the statistics and the discs of importance, but also WHY these musicians, this group, at that time, managed to capture the imagination of the young, and later, older generations, in every country where music is played. It analyses Merseybeat and why one British city spawned such a harvest of successful performers; it looks at the role of Brian Epstein, the man who steered the Beatles to the top. It gives a blow-by-blow account of the internal agonies that led to the eventual split. And, to complete this intimate biography, it records the individual careers of the ex-Beatles, showing that the world did not lose a great group but gained four major superstars.

First published 1975 by
Octopus Books Limited
59 Grosvenor Street, London W1

© 1973/1974/1975
Phoebus Publishing Company.

Some of the material has been previously published in another form. The book is produced by Phoebus Publishing Company in cooperation with Octopus Books Limited
ISBN 0 7064 0446 7

Produced by
Mandarin Publishers Limited
22a Westlands Road Quarry Bay,
Hong Kong
Printed in Hong Kong

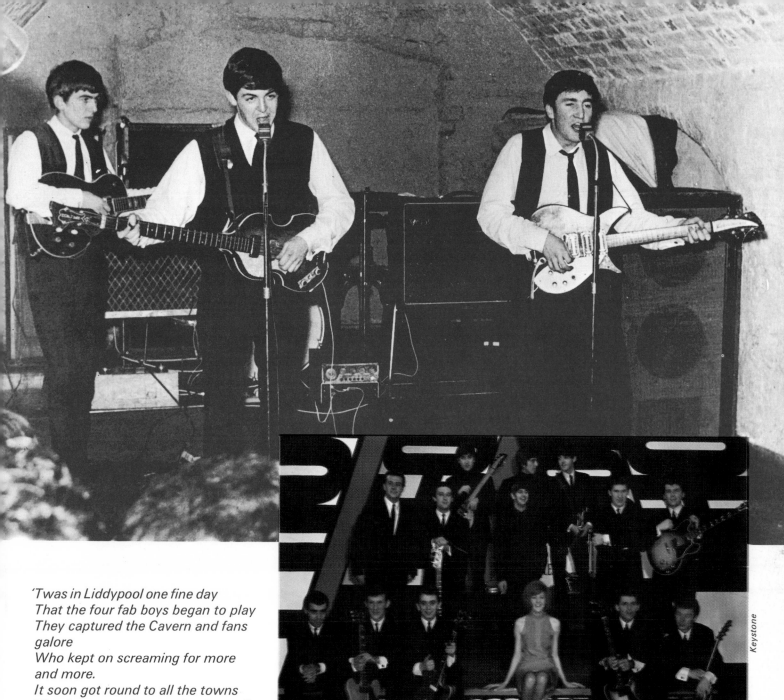

*'Twas in Liddypool one fine day
That the four fab boys began to play
They captured the Cavern and fans galore
Who kept on screaming for more and more.
It soon got round to all the towns
That here was the sound to beat all sounds.'*

(reader's letter in **The Beatles Book**, *March 1965*)

Top: George, Paul and John on stage at the Cavern. Above: Merseysound stars Billy J. Kramer and the Dakotas (left), the Beatles, Cilla Black and the Searchers (right).

The Mersey Sound

That of course is the legend — the Beatles created Merseybeat all by themselves. The reality was rather different. From 1959 to 1962, when their first record, 'Love Me Do', was a minor hit which established them as the top Liverpool group, they were just one of a dozen bands who stood out from the 300 or so performing regularly on Merseyside.

There was Kingsize Taylor and the Dominoes, who always claimed to have been the first Liverpool beat group; Cass and the Casanovas (later the Big Three), who always disputed that claim; Rory Storme and the Hurricanes, whose drummer, Ringo Starr, sat in with the Beatles during their second trip to Hamburg in 1961; Derry Wilkie and the Seniors, the first Mersey group to play in Germany; the Chants, the first all-black vocal group in the country; Freddie Starr and the Midnighters (whose leader became a successful TV comedian), and Faron's Flamingos. All these groups were big names within Liverpool itself, while others became known nationally in the wake of the Beatles' success: Gerry and the Pacemakers; Billy J. Kramer and the Dakotas; the Merseybeats; the Swinging Blue Jeans; and the Searchers.

These groups all played at dozens of venues up and down Merseyside. The famous Cavern was a Trad jazz club until May 25th, 1960, when its first beat session featured Rory Storme and the Hurricanes, with Cass and the Casanovas. Its main rivals were the Jacaranda (which like the Cavern was managed by Alan Williams, the Beatles' first manager), where the walls were decorated with murals by Stuart Sutcliffe, the Beatles' first bass player; and the Iron Door, home of the Searchers.

Outside the city centre there were ball-

Keystone   J. Allan Cash   Pictorial Press

Top left: The early Beatles — Stuart Sutcliffe, Paul, George and Pete Best. Centre: With Liverpool behind — the Beatles, Gerry and t

rooms, church halls, and civic halls like Litherland Town Hall, Aintree Institute, Wilson Hall in Garston, and the Jive Hive at Crosby. There was a Merseybeat boat trip to the Isle of Man, with over a dozen groups on board. Special events were held at local venues like New Brighton Pier, where Rory Storme once climbed on top of the Pavilion and broke his leg falling through the glass roof. Liverpool could also claim to have pioneered pop festivals when on one occasion 14 hours of music from 25 groups was presented at Stanley Stadium — tickets cost a pound.

A Little More Money

Before the Beatles and Gerry had their hits no musicians on Merseyside made much money. Five pounds a night was about average, and at one period the Beatles got just five shillings each for playing at the Jacaranda. Nearly every group was semi-professional, and most got their equipment through credit contracts guaranteed by their parents. A lot of the beat groups grew out of street gangs in working-class areas like the Dingle — kids

who'd been enthralled by *Rock Around The Clock*, and wanted to do more than dance or slash seats to rock & roll music.

For the top Liverpool groups, though, Hamburg soon became *the* place to play and earn a little more money. According to Alan Williams, the German connection came about almost accidentally, when a Hamburg club owner came to Liverpool and poached a steel band who were booked at the Jacaranda. In the negotiations which followed he persuaded the Germans that what they needed was an English beat group. A summer season in Blackpool for Howie Casey and the Seniors had just fallen through, so Williams shipped them off to the Kaiser Keller club. They were a howling success, so soon afterwards, the Beatles too appeared in Hamburg, at the Indra.

The Hamburg experience was the making of the Beatles and nearly every Mersey group who played there. Having to play long sets, in an environment where they knew only each other, welded the groups together into tight units. They also had to modify their style to the raucous drinking and dancing clubs of the Reeper-

bahn. The groups had to concentrate on loud, rocking numbers: ''At the beginning they (the Beatles) still played a lot of the Shadows' numbers, but gradually turned to R&B with such numbers as 'Roll Over Beethoven','' recalled Howie Casey.

The German audiences also wanted groups who were visually exciting. They would call out for the musicians to 'mak show', and the Beatles, in particular, responded. A German booking-agent later described some of their stunts:

''John Lennon marched in one night wearing just bathing trunks. Once, too, a toilet seat mysteriously disappeared from the club. Sure enough, John appeared with it round his neck like some wooden horse-shoe. The boys didn't mind taking the risk of upsetting the local people. They'd ape Hitler and do the goose-step. And of course the local fans soon learnt to love them . . .''
(from Billy Shepherd's The True Story of the Beatles.)

An important element in the development of the Liverpool music scene was the newspaper, *Mersey Beat*, edited by Bill Harry who had studied magazine design

10

...acemakers, Billy J. Kramer and the Dakotas and Brian Epstein. Top right: The Big Three, with Gerry and the Pacemakers below.

at the Art College where both John Lennon and Stuart Sutcliffe had been. From the first issue John was a regular contributor and many of his humorous pieces ended up in his book *In His Own Write*. It was the winning of the *Mersey Beat* poll in 1962 which finally established the Beatles as the top Liverpool group.

Despite all this intense activity, nobody outside Merseyside knew what was happening there until Brian Epstein finally managed to interest George Martin in his Beatles tapes. The recording industry, in the UK, was centred on London, and as long as Cliff Richard and the Shadows, Billy Fury and Bobby Vee kept on selling records, it wasn't interested in local groups from provincial towns.

Colourless Sound

The Liverpool groups had a similar lack of interest in the hit parade music of 1959–62. They had grown up with the rock & roll music of Chuck Berry and Little Richard, next to which most of the early '60s stuff sounded pretty colourless. Besides, they had access to contemporary

rhythm & blues hits from the States — thanks to Liverpool's situation as a seaport. Merchant seamen returning from New York would bring back records by such people as the Contours, the Miracles, Barrett Strong and Barbara George for their friends or brothers in the beat groups. Add to that the musical heritage of Liverpool in terms of folk music and country & western (Bill Harry estimates that there were 40 country groups operating on Merseyside in the heyday of beat music), and you can see what a rich mixture of popular music the groups had to draw on forming their own individual styles.

Even among the rock & roll numbers they chose to perform, the best Merseybeat groups picked out the unusual. There were several recordings of songs written by the Coasters' producers, Mike Leiber and Jerry Stoller, with their witty lyrics and singalong choruses notably 'What About Us' by the Undertakers, and 'Thumbin' A Ride' by Earl Preston and the T.T.s. Those qualities were also apparent in the R&B songs that became Merseybeat standards without anybody else in the country, except a few collectors, having ever

heard them. There was 'Some Other Guy', recorded by the Big Three after Liverpool was 'discovered' by the metropolitan record companies; 'Fortune Teller' (originally done by the New Orleans singer Aaron Neville, and put on record in Britain by the Merseybeats); 'Do You Love Me' (the Contours' song with which Brian Poole defeated Faron's Flamingos for the British hit); and the well-known 'Money' and 'Twist And Shout'.

The Liverpool groups didn't practice sexual discrimination in the slower numbers they performed. The Shirelles' 'Baby It's You' was popular, Little Eva's 'Let's Turkey Trot' and 'Our Day Will Come' by Ruby and the Romantics were covered on record by Mersey groups in 1963. Otherwise, the beat groups were surprisingly conventional in their quieter material — adopting songs from musical shows, and standard ballads like 'You'll Never Walk Alone' and 'Till There Was You'.

Because nearly all the records made by Liverpool groups, after they had been signed by major record companies, were hastily and unimaginatively produced in the hope of leaping on the Beatles band-

11

MERSEYSIDE'S OWN ENTERTAINMENTS PAPER

MERSEY Beat

CRANES

The name for
Records, Amplifiers
Transistor Radios
Also Pianos
and Organs

HANOVER STREET, LIVERPOOL 1
Telephone: ROYal 4714

NEMS

WHITECHAPEL AND GREAT
CHARLOTTE STREET

*THE FINEST RECORD SELEC-
TIONS IN THE NORTH*

Open until 6-0 p.m. each day
(Thursday and Saturday 6-30 p.m.)

Vol. 1 No. 13   JANUARY 4-18, 1962   Price THREEPENCE

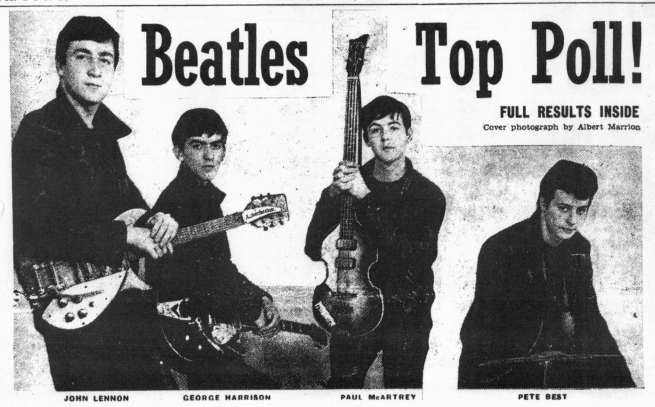

Beatles Top Poll!

FULL RESULTS INSIDE
Cover photograph by Albert Marrion

JOHN LENNON   GEORGE HARRISON   PAUL McARTREY   PETE BEST

wagon, it's very difficult to realise how exciting Merseybeat was in its natural habitat. There were, however, a few records made in Liverpool itself which captured some of the feeling of the music. Bill Harry has since described that feeling as "the voice of musicians in love with their instruments and the yells of the audiences who were up there with them."

Recognition At Last

One of these is an EP called 'The Big Three Live At The Cavern'. On it you can hear how the good-humoured shouting and whistling of the audience was almost part of the Mersey sound. The excitement is increased because the musicians aren't total masters of their instruments; you can hear, in the way they play, the enthusiasm and effort that went into Merseybeat. It's all very different from the 'cool', effortless approach of the Shadows, and the immaculate production jobs on records by American singers of the time like Neil Sedaka and Johnny Tillotson. The two albums called 'This Is Mersey Beat' recorded in Liverpool by John Schroeder of Oriole, a now defunct record company, convey the same excitement

through the work of a large number of Liverpool groups. All these records have been unavailable for a number of years, but happily United Artists have recently acquired many of them for a new double-album of the Mersey sound.

Although the Beatles were part of Merseybeat, there were also important things which differentiated them from the other Liverpool groups. While most musicians composed the occasional song, Lennon and McCartney wrote continually and consistently — they had nearly 100 songs written before they made their first record. This songwriting ability and interest must have owed a lot to the semi-bohemian, art college background of John Lennon and Stuart Sutcliffe. In addition, the vocal harmonies worked out by the Beatles were more sophisticated than those of nearly every other group in Liverpool. They had obviously listened carefully to early Tamla groups like the Miracles, as well as the Everly Brothers and the Drifters. They had learned how to use harmonies to give songs their own pace — the slow build-up to a climax — something that rock & roll and rhythm & blues weren't too concerned with. 'You Really Gotta Hold On Me' is a good

example of the Beatles' early grasp of this.

But of course, the immediate reason that the Beatles were the first Liverpool group to reach out to audiences beyond Lancashire and Hamburg was Brian Epstein. And it was ironic, if inevitable, that the moment Epstein persuaded George Martin to sign the group marked the beginning of the end for Merseybeat as a living music. For as soon as 'Please Please Me' and Gerry and the Pacemakers' 'How Do You Do It?' were hits, record company scouts descended on Merseyside like a plague of locusts. Any group with any talent, and some with none, was signed. Hardly any of them were recorded by anyone with the same understanding of their music that George Martin had of Epstein's stable of groups. Most made a couple of singles (often of rock or R&B numbers), had their brief hour of glory, and caught the train home.

The live music scene in Liverpool was devastated. Not only had the mature groups been whisked away, but so had the next generation of musicians who had yet to master their craft. Although it was only in 1973 that the Cavern finally closed, Merseybeat on Merseyside was dead by 1965.

The Beatle Years 1956–1970

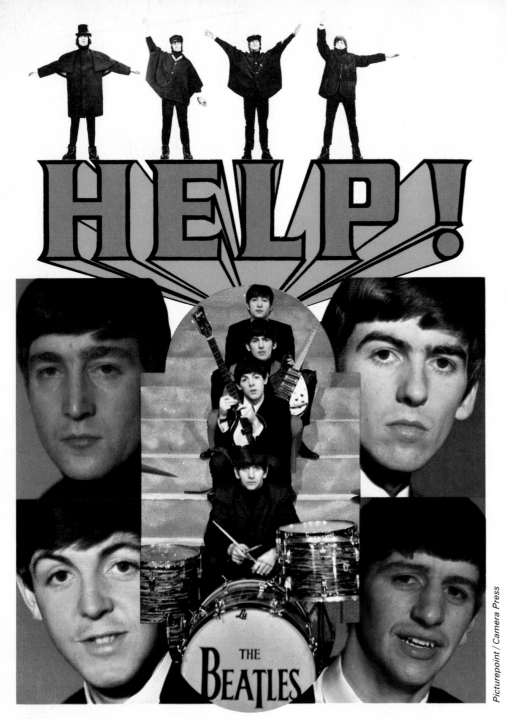

HELP!

Pictorial Press

Above, from L to R: Semaphore publicity for the Beatles' film *Help!*. Two pictures of the Fab Four on stage in America. Displaying their hard-earned MBEs. On stage in Britain with, below, a typical Beatles' publicity picture of the mid-'60s.

Picturepoint / Camera Press

Ringo Starr once said that he'd like to end up 'sort of unforgettable'. Well, it's an ambition he certainly achieved, and with the possible exception of Presley, the Beatles — several years after their final split — still remain the most illustrious, influential, and potent names in the history of rock.

For a large part of the '60s, the Beatles were possibly the most famous men in the world. There is no way in which their all-powerful, all-embracing domination of the music scene from 1963–67 can be adequately described. In those years just to say 'The Beatles' was enough. To anyone who was over 10 and under 30 in those heady days of the '60s, the Beatles meant more than songs, performances and records: they meant a life-style, dress, slang, attitudes, humour and hair. They created a culture. Boys from London to Los Angeles, from Berlin to Tokyo wore button-down shirts, knitted ties and Cuban-heeled boots. The faithful imitators drank whisky and coke, and smoked Lark cigarettes. Everyone grew their hair. If you weren't Beatle-ish you were out of it.

The story of the Beatles rise from the back-streets of Liverpool, through Hamburg

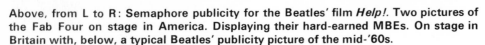

BACK TRACK

July, 1940	:	Ringo Starr born.
October, 1940	:	John Lennon born.
June, 1942	:	Paul McCartney born.
February, 1943	:	George Harrison born.
1956	:	John forms the Quarrymen skiffle group.
June	:	Paul meets John, joins the Quarrymen.
1958	:	George joins the Quarrymen.
1959	:	John, George, Paul and Stuart Sutcliffe become the Silver Beatles. Audition for Larry Parnes who offers them two-week tour of Scotland as backing group.
1960	:	Pete Best joins group as drummer. Group play Liverpool clubs. First trip to Hamburg.
1961	:	Residency at the Cavern Club, Liverpool.
April	:	Second trip to Hamburg. Record with Tony Sheridan.
June	:	Return to Liverpool leaving Sutcliffe in Hamburg.
October	:	Boy walks into NEMS record store in Liverpool, asks manager Brian Epstein for disc called 'My Bonnie' by the Beatles.
November	:	Brian Epstein meets Beatles.
December	:	Brian Epstein signs Beatles.
1962		
January	:	Beatles audition for Decca.
March	:	Decca turns down group followed by Pye, Columbia, HMV and EMI.
April	:	Third trip to Hamburg.
May	:	Epstein meets George Martin.
June	:	Group auditions for Martin.

Associated Press   Associated Press   Pictorial Press   Syndication International

and via the London Palladium to the world, is far too well-known and well-documented to need repetition. By 1968, a bare six years after the release of 'Love Me Do', they had their own fat and official biography — not to mention the unofficial and boot-legged versions. There can't be anyone now listening to rock who is not at least aware of the skeleton of the history. They've been analysed from every obvious and several obscure angles; they've been compared to almost anyone you can think of; they've been called the greatest songwriters since Schubert; they've been scrutinised in publications ranging from teenybopper weeklies to the London *Times*. The Beatles are simply the best documented, best loved, most celebrated rock group the world has ever seen. And while others have since matched and even bettered their record sales in a year, vied for their honours, and commanded the same intense and fervent following, no one has yet come close to equalling the universal popularity of the band.

The question that has nagged commentators since the first flowerings of their success (1963 in Britain, '64 in America and thence the world) is why? Why these four young men? What did they have that no one else could muster? What was the chemistry that Lennon, McCartney,

Harrison and Starr created that produced so violent, spontaneous and widespread a reaction? To try and analyse their history is rather like trying to define magic. The obvious word that springs to the lips is 'charisma' — now so over-used, so misused, as to be almost meaningless. But charisma it is, for charisma is a personal quality or gift that enables an individual to impress and influence many of his fellows. In the Beatles' case, millions.

Beatle Games

There are the usual Beatle games that have been played. Games like: would they ever have made it individually? An old game. Could Laurel have made it without Hardy? Astaire without Rogers? The short answer is no. Or, taken a step further, could the Beatles have made it without Harrison, or McCartney? Again, no. They didn't make it without Ringo. Certainly both Lennon and McCartney would have done *something;* a songwriting talent like that couldn't have gone unnoticed. Certainly, since the split, they've all continued successfully — but that was in the wake of the Beatles. The group was the *sine qua non.* Without it there would be no 'Imagine', no Wings, no 'Something'. Arguably there would have been no Rolling Stones, no

Bowie — nothing that youth is today. The fact is that you just cannot understate the effect the Beatles had, not only on their own generation and several younger ones, but also their parents.

By the same token, it is hard to overstate their influence. They may or may not be the greatest songwriters since Schubert, but who cares anyway? The Beatles burst on to a generation like Sun Gods. Their enormous dazzling presence blazed a trail that turned the course of music and, without the slightest exaggeration, the century. In their wake the attitudes, manners and morals of the young and many of their elders were radically changed. What they didn't accomplish themselves (and that was a great deal musically, in fashion and in life-style), they acted as a spearhead for, and opened the way to others. Once the Beatles had trodden the path and shown the way there was hardly a kid in Europe or North America who didn't believe that he could follow. Suddenly it really was possible that you could become rich and/or famous as a writer, musician, hair stylist, fashion designer, model, actor or a whole range of associated skills. What the Beatles did, very nearly single-handed, was put the entire emphasis on youth.

But, the question remains — why them? Why four working-class lads from

August	:	Pete Best sacked, Ringo Starr offered drummer's job with group.	May	:	Third national tour of Britain with Roy Orbison. Start of screaming and riots.
September	:	First recording session at EMI.	June	:	'Twist and Shout' EP reaches no. 1.
October	:	'Love Me Do' released.	August	:	'She Loves You' no. 1. Advance orders of 500,000 for disc.
December	:	'Love Me Do' enters UK charts: highest position 17. Fourth trip to Hamburg.	September	:	'The Beatles Hits' EP.
1963			October	:	Booked to play major UK TV spectacular, *Sunday Night At The London Palladium.* Theatre mobbed by fans all day. Start of 'Beatlemania'. Tour of Sweden. On their return to London Airport they encountered the first of the many riotous welcomes that were to follow them around the world.
January	:	'Please Please Me' released; reaches no. 1.			
February	:	First national tour of Britain; Helen Shapiro tops bill.			
March	:	Second national tour of Britain; Beatles third on bill under Chris Montez and Tommy Roe. Gerry and the Pacemakers top charts with 'How Do You Do It'; start of 'Liverpool Sound'.			
April	:	'From Me To You' no. 1. Release first album: 'Please Please Me'.	November	:	Appear at *Royal Variety Show* before Queen Elizabeth the Queen Mother, Princess Margaret and Lord Snowdon. Beginning of acceptance by show business

Syndication International

Keystone Press

Liverpool? There were a number of important factors, and all have to do with what makes a star. True stars usually have a number of things in common. And by stars we're really talking in terms of the monsters that Hollywood produced in its heyday; those personalities so glittering and huge that they dwarf all but a few that rock has ever produced. The truly *GREAT* stars combine a number of factors. They are always true to themselves no matter what publicity bandwagon, what pressures, what crises, what images have tried to do to them — they are fundamentally honest. Bogart had it. In every film he was,

essentially, Bogie; his own man, secure and confident in himself. So were the Beatles. Whatever excesses were heaped on them they still remained true to themselves — four totally individual people. MBE's, Establishment blandishments, royalty, showbiz glitter or near-Godlike worship never shook them out of their true personalities. They could walk through it all, shrug it off, use it, turn it to advantage or mock it, but they always remained — however tenuously — in control. It never swamped them: and therefore it never destroyed them.

Their appeal was bi-sexual; they attracted both sexes equally but differently.

continued from previous page

establishment. MP asks questions in House of Commons about number of policemen taken off other duties because of Beatlemania. Fourth UK tour, this time with top billing. Start of merchandising of Beatle products. London *Daily Telegraph* compares hysteria with Hitler mass rallies. Mob scenes wherever group appears. 'With The Beatles' album released; 250,000 advance orders for it, highest in history, overtaking 200,000 for Presley's best — 'Blue Hawaii'. Fifth single, 'I Want To Hold Your Hand' released; direct to no. 1, advance orders of one million.

December   : Seven records — singles and EPs — in Top Twenty. Film plans announced. British fan club tops 80,000 members. Appear in

Beatles Christmas Show in London. London *Times* music critic names them 'outstanding English composers of 1963'. *Sunday Times* critic declares them 'greatest composers since Beethoven'.

1964

January   : 'I Want To Hold Your Hand' enters US charts at no. 83. Play Olympia Theatre, Paris. First concert coolly received. 'She Loves You' enters US charts; 'I Want To Hold Your Hand' top in States; 'Please Please Me' LP enters album charts. Intensive US nationwide publicity campaign mounted to prelude first visit.

February   : Beatles arrival at Kennedy Airport attracts screaming crowds in excess of 10,000. Top billing on *Ed Sullivan Show*. 50,000

London Features

Camera Press

Kobal Collection

While girls screamed, boys applauded. While females loved, males admired. While women yearned, men imitated. Both the personalities and the music appealed to the two sexes, and each Beatle had such an individual persona that he could be adopted for different reasons by different people. Simply, Ringo was cuddly, Paul was beautiful, John was strong and faintly intellectual, George was spiritual, ethereal. Their appeal likewise crossed all barriers. Initially they were *for* and *of* the kids; but once they had been firmly adopted by the under 30s they broadened and charmed the mums and dads alike. The older folks who hated their hair loved 'Yesterday' and 'All My Loving'. It was admitted generally that they had talent and could turn a good tune.

The four Beatles were extraordinarily ordinary — or ordinary in a most extraordinary way. They talked in an accent that was off the street; wrote songs that were seemingly so simple; and sang well, but without any vocal pyrotechnics. It was all a deception, of course. The songs appeared simple but they were cleverly and intriguingly constructed. The first few seemed too easy for words but were, in fact, tautly and beautifully pared to the

		apply for 728 available seats. 73,000,000 watch broadcast. Concert at Washington's Coliseum in front of 20,000 crowd followed by fracas at British Embassy. Two concerts at Carnegie Hall, both sell-outs. Second *Ed Sullivan Show.* On return to London, Prime Minister calls them 'our best exports'. 'All My Loving' EP makes no. 13.
March	:	Lennon's book *In His Own Write* published; heads best seller list. 'Can't Buy Me Love' released and is an instant no. 1 in UK and States with advance sales of 3,000,000. Start filming *A Hard Day's Night.* George meets Pattie Boyd.
Summer		'Long Tall Sally' EP makes no. 11. Tours of Europe, Hong Kong, Australia and New Zealand. Biggest ever crowd turns out to see

		Beatles arrive in Adelaide — estimated in excess of 300,000.
July	:	*A Hard Day's Night* premiered in London. Warm critical reception. Record of title song makes no. 1, and album reaches no. 22.
August September	:	First major US tour, 31 performances in 24 cities. All existing attendance, fee and grossing records smashed.
November	:	'I Feel Fine' makes no. 1.
December	:	'Beatles For Sale' LP.
1965		
April	:	'Ticket To Ride' reaches no. 1.
June	:	Announcement of award to Beatles of MBEs. Storm of protest including House of Lords and return of awards by holders. Medals sent back from all over the world.
August	:	US tour including concert at Shea Stadium,

bone; and 'Please Please Me' instantly made the ears prick up with a chord sequence that sounded so odd. The song didn't proceed as expected but dipped and soared, bending and weaving in an intriguing way that teased the memory when you tried to whistle it. And the singing was not the usual slavish dependence on a limited range, as with the majority of other artists whose faces and carefully nurtured images meant more than their vocal ability. They were the classic local boys making good, the boys-next-door or down the street. But while their backgrounds were ordinary, their talent and their personalities were certainly not. Nonetheless, any Joe could dream that, given the breaks and the luck, he too could be a Beatle.

Grotty And Gear

The Beatles were stylish. There was a uniqueness and exclusivity about them that comes from people who work long and hard together; who build up their own private language and humour; who dress, act, talk and play to please themselves and each other rather than society. They were a club, a gang, a clique. They talked differently; were happy to use their own slang like 'fab' and 'grotty' and 'gear'; they were irreverent, slightly bizarre. They dressed modishly, but with an individualism that was carefully groomed and polished by Epstein. And everyone wants to be an insider, so that once the Beatles' individuality had been recognised everyone wanted to join the select few. A generation slavishly followed them as one — in fashion, in language, in every tiny detail. If a Beatle wore his tie only half knotted, without tucking the long end through the knot, you knew that within the week hundreds of

thousands would follow. If a Beatle wore funny little round glasses, you knew that within the month an industry had started.

Perhaps the most important reason why *they* carried all before was that, like all true stars, they were the right people with the right goods at the right time. And that's something on the wind, in the mood of the age; a visceral rather than cerebral feeling that defies analysis. The Beatles were so uniquely of the '60s, as Presley was of the '50s, that any study of the decade — however learned — cannot ignore them. To say that they dominated the style and music of the decade and profoundly influenced almost everything that was to follow is almost to state the obvious. A proof of their quality, if any is needed, is the way their music holds up. In the years between 1963 and '69 they released a dozen albums, the vast majority of the songs on which were composed by Lennon and McCartney. Listening to them today one is struck by the consistently high standard they achieved: few songs have dated, few sound tired or hackneyed; the majority are fresh, original and highly individual.

In retrospect, however, it is difficult to recall the extent of the adulation the Beatles enjoyed. They dominated the media, were drooled over by personalities, the public, the press and politicians alike. They were the 'Moptops' to the press, the boys to the fans, and dollar-earners to the British Government. They were accosted by scissor-wielding, souvenir-grabbing ladies of society at the British Embassy in Washington, embraced by the then-Prime Minister Harold Wilson, courted, feted and idolised everywhere. And at the bedrock was the near-worship of fans by the million. Wherever they went they were met by terrifying mob scenes. Their arrival in the States — the most important

jumping-off ground they could ever encounter — was signalled by a $50,000 'crash publicity programme' which, as one executive of their record company commented, 'was a lot of hype'. He went on to point out that 'all the hype in the world isn't going to sell a bad product'. He was right, of course, and the hype worked. 50,000 people applied for tickets to their *Ed Sullivan Show*. Carnegie Hall was a sell-out. It was a famous victory.

Big Brother

It was famous largely because no other British artist had managed to conquer the home of rock. The British had a deep-rooted musical inferiority complex. Rock & roll had been born in the States, it had toddled there, grown there, and then it had invaded Europe. Until quite late into the '50s British rock and pop were pale imitations of Big Brother across the Atlantic. Few British artists had ever made a showing in the charts — Britain's biggest star, Cliff Richard, hadn't even managed to make a dent. British fans were so used to seeing their charts dominated by Americans, her musicians reconciled to following where transatlantic artists led, that no one, including the Beatles themselves, could really believe that they had anything to offer.

Their success gave not only themselves but a whole nation confidence. Suddenly the entire emphasis shifted to London, to the Swinging London mythology of *Life* magazine. It was almost as if Britain had won the war again. After their barn-storming victories in the States nothing was impossible. There were no heights they couldn't reach; they had the Midas touch, it seemed. Everything they touched turned to gold. They took a crack at films,

continued from previous page
	New York, before an audience of over 55,000. $304,000 taken claimed as biggest gross in show business history. 'Help' movie and album released.	
December	: 'We Can Work It Out' tenth consecutive hit to be instant no. 1 in UK. 'Beatles Million Sellers' EP. 'Rubber Soul'. Includes 'Norwegian Wood', first sign of George's growing interest in India is in the use of the sitar. Commence tour of Britain which, although not announced, is to be their last.	

1966
May	: Last live appearance in Britain at Wembley.
June	: 'Paperback Writer' is the first single in over two years not to jump straight to the top of the British charts. It eventually did reach the no. 1 position. World tour includes Japan.
August	: John is quoted in a newspaper as saying that the 'Beatles are now more popular than Christ'. Causes furore in States; Ku Klux Klan burn effigies of the group. Last US tour and biggest grosser. Final live appearance anywhere in the world in San Francisco, 29th August. 'Yellow Submarine'/'Eleanor Rigby' released. 'Revolver' includes the first hint of drug influences on 'Tomorrow Never Knows'.

September	: George and Patti Harrison visit India. John appears with Dick Lester in the film *How I Won The War*.

1967
February	: The Harrisons' first contact with the Maharishi. This interest in the mysticism of the East, coupled with acid, greatly influenced the rest of the year. The Beatles now completely retired from personal appearances and touring. All work from here is in studios. 'Penny Lane'/'Strawberry Fields' released; first single since 'Love Me Do' to fail to reach no. 1.
June	: 'Sgt Pepper's Lonely Hearts Club Band' released. 'A Day In The Life' banned by BBC and some US stations because of alleged overt drug allusions.
July	: Appear on world-wide TV programme *Our World* singing 'All You Need Is Love'. Seen by estimated 150,000,000 viewers. Song released as single and makes no. 1.
August	: Brian Epstein commits suicide while the Beatles attend a course given by the Maharishi in Wales.
November	: 'Hello Goodbye' released.
December	: *Magical Mystery Tour* TV film judged a failure by critics. Described as 'witless' and 'blatant rubbish'. Plans for Apple announced and shop

Camera Press

"The thing is, we're all really the same person. We're just four parts of the one." – Paul

Mike Cook

and *Hard Day's Night* met with warm critical success. There just wasn't a sour note for three glorious years.

The greatest tribute to the Beatles is that when the going was this good their standards never dropped – indeed their music got better and better. Single after single flew straight to the top of the charts, and each new album capped the last in originality. They managed, it seemed, to avoid all the pitfalls that Elvis had plunged into: their only two films were both of high quality, and they never went soft, musically. Just when one of Paul's sweet ballads seemed to be the trend John came out with something freaky, or George floated off in a new direction – even introducing a new culture to the West. When it seemed like they'd finally sold out by accepting official honours at Buckingham Palace, they were into drugs and puzzling lyrics. For five years they never stopped moving.

Probably the first sign that they weren't infallible came at Christmas 1967, when BBC TV in Britain screened *Magical Mystery Tour*, the group's first self-made film.

It was labelled by the critics as non-sensical and over-indulgent. It certainly wasn't very good, but the beating it took may in part be explained as a backlash. The Golden Boys had had it too good for too long, and now was the time for their come-uppance. Slowly, from that point on, the tide began to turn. They weathered the *Magical Mystery Tour* storm, and their major abilities in writing and performing were unimpaired. But the next two years saw changes.

The group were maturing as individuals and starting to grow apart. Epstein's death certainly had an effect, as did the episode with the Maharishi, George's continuing involvement with India and things spiritual, and John's relationship with Yoko Ono which took him on to newer horizons.

It was inevitable that they should go their own ways. In fact, it was probably desirable. The unpleasantness surrounding business interests, and the bickering over management were sad and ultimately destructive, but they were probably only the public side of conflicts that went much deeper. It is conceivable that even despite the tensions the Beatles would have split anyway because, just as they were supremely children of their time and flourished during that era, their impeccable sense of timing would have told them when enough was enough. They got out when they were still on top. They suffered no sorry decline into obscurity or second-rate billing, living off the glories of the past.

Whatever the reason, the Beatles' retirement from the arena marked the end of an extraordinary era – one they had themselves created. They were still stars; they are stars now and, to some generations anyway, they will always be stars. They were in the end, as they had been throughout, true to themselves. Sort of unforgettable.

		opened. 'Magical Mystery Tour' album released.
1968		
February	:	Studying in India with the Maharishi: John and George for two months, Paul for one, Ringo for 10 days. Many plans announced for Apple during the early part of the year.
March	:	'Lady Madonna' released (no. 1).
June	:	John's marriage to Cynthia breaks down, he is seen openly with Yoko Ono.
July	:	The cartoon film *Yellow Submarine* is premiered.
August	:	Apple shop suddenly closed.
September	:	'Hey Jude' the Beatles' first release on the new Apple label (no. 1).
November	:	The Beatles 'white' album is released. Also, John and Yoko's 'Two Virgins' with a cover picture of them both in the nude.
1969		
January	:	Filming of *Let It Be* started. Rifts between John and Paul widening.
February	:	Allen Klein appointed as their adviser.
March	:	Paul marries Linda Eastman. John marries Yoko Ono.
April	:	'Get Back' topped the charts.
May	:	'The Ballad Of John And Yoko' (no. 1).
July	:	Plastic Ono Band releases 'Give Peace A Chance'.

August	:	'Abbey Road', the Beatles' last album, recorded. Linda gives birth to Paul's first daughter, Mary.
October	:	Plastic Ono Band releases 'Cold Turkey'. George Harrison's 'Something' makes no. 2 for the Beatles.
November	:	John returns his MBE as a protest against Britain's involvement in the wars in Biafra and Vietnam.
1970		
February	:	Plastic Ono Band releases 'Instant Karma'.
April	:	Paul issues a home-made album of his own songs entitled 'McCartney'.
May	:	Premier of the film *Let It Be* but none of the Beatles turned up. The Beatles became artistically independent of each other. Ringo releases his album 'Sentimental Journey'.
September	:	Ringo's next release, 'Beaucoup Of Blues'. George brings out his album 'All Things Must Pass'.
December	:	John releases an album entitled 'John Lennon' by John Lennon/Plastic Ono Band. Paul files a court suit demanding the dissolution of the Beatles, and the appointment of a receiver.

"I didn't leave the Beatles. The Beatles have left the Beatles – but no one wants to be the one to say the party's over." – Paul

Beatlemania

Pandemonium at airports, stage-doors and hotels is nothing new to pop. Since the days of Valentino, whose funeral route was lined by thousands of sobbing women, hysteria and emotional excesses have gone hand in hand with stardom. The kind of devotion and acclaim that used to be lavished on European dictators is now commonplace every time some of todays' superstars make a move. To airport authorities who have to cope with mobs of teenyboppers greeting the arrival of an Osmond or a Cassidy, the whole thing must seem rather small-time. Ten years before, these same people were at the centre of Beatlemania, and nothing before or since has ever come close to equalling that particular emotional epidemic.

To catalogue Beatlemania exactly for anyone who wasn't there would be impossible. Even the memory is pale in comparison with reality, and if it happened again now it would still amaze everyone all over again. Spend a day looking through newspaper files, watch a week of news film, read a dozen of the thousands of books they inspired, and you won't begin to know the half of what it was like. Travel back in time and live in the midst of it and it's a trip into bedlam. Not just a few screaming girls, but the whole world seemingly gone mad. The cause of it all was four lads from Liverpool – John, Paul, George and Ringo.

No one has yet managed to define the phenomenon. Psychologists have pored over it with long words, historians have picked at it, critics have analysed it endlessly. Probably not since Shakespeare has so much intellect been invested in explaining something so simple. The Beatles were four guys in a pop group who made happy music and gave everyone a good time for a few years. Far more will be read into their lyrics and their success than was ever there to start with, and if the world continues that long, schoolkids a 100 or so years from now will probably read about major events that have influenced the course of history: the Black Death in the Middle Ages, Beatlemania in the mid-'60s.

In the beginning the Beatles, or rather the Quarrymen, were just another group who hoped to make a few records and

some money. They showed little talent and no particular sparkle. Clubs didn't rush to book them. Decca and Pye turned them down. They toured with Helen Shapiro, and she was the star. Then, as with even the greatest talent, luck stepped in. Someone was due to make it big, but what might have been a huge and hasty success for someone else, turned into something more because it happened to those particular four people.

It all started with them being so ordinary. Theatre and cinema were at last turning to reality. The 'working-class hero' of *Saturday Night and Sunday Morning* and *The Loneliness of the Long-Distance Runner* was ready to move into music. Being working-class, being like the majority who bought records only more so, was a start. It was almost as though the Beatles were being rich and successful on behalf of everyone else. There's an American novel, *Dando Shaft,* in which the hero advertises for a million people to each give him a dollar: he is the people's millionaire who lives out the fantasies of luxury for them all. It was as if the Beatles had come up on the horses for every man, woman and child; and instead of retiring to a no-publicity bungalow by the sea, they let everyone share the win. They stayed nice, normal, modest and funny.

To see film of their early days with neat haircuts and uniform clothes and listen to their first hum-along songs is to know that now they wouldn't rate a second glance. They hadn't the glitter of Presley

Mirrorpic

Syndication International

These pictures show the effects that the Beatles had on their fans, wherever they went.

Central Press Photos

or the glamour of Monroe. They were buses not cars, semi- not detached, sink not bath, but they truly belonged to their fans.

One other great point in their favour was that they were not just four people, but four 'personalities'. John was the thinker, Paul the romantic, George the mystic and Ringo the clown, and they were all lovable. Something for everyone in fact. No one but an ardent Osmond fan could tell you the names of all the brothers, but John, George, Paul and Ringo were on the lips of grannies, toddlers, Kings and kids the world over. Whether they approved or disapproved of the mass stupidity, either way no one could help knowing all about the cause of it, and mostly the response was a world-wide thumbs-up of approval.

Compared To Hitler

Girls went to their concerts, wept un-controllably, covered their ears and screamed through the music. Beside them men and boys shouted with an energy normally reserved only for football matches. Sunday papers wrote in-depth features. In Britain the *Daily Telegraph* compared them to Hitler, 'filling empty heads with hysteria' and *The Daily Worker* said they were the voice of '300,000 people on the Dole'. Elvis, Cassius Clay and Prince Philip all commented generously on them. Politicians fell over themselves to mention them in their speeches, and Harold Wilson even

sought popular favour by arranging, in June 1965, that they should be awarded the MBE for services to the country's economy.

Imagine this happening to Slade or the Sweet. Imagine Marc Bolan being knighted, and you might have some idea how far Beatlemania went. In the States kids carried banners saying 'Ringo For President'. In Britain, the Beatles could probably have formed a government.

The Beatles were everywhere. Their records decorated the most elegant coffee tables, as well as the grottiest apartments. They were in everything – books, maga-zines, posters, fashions. There were Beatle suits, cut in the style of their favourite stage outfits – jackets with soft mandarin collars. Beatle wigs sold like hot cakes, and covered every kind of male head from military short-back-and-sides to the middle-aged bald. Factories started insisting on hair-nets for male workers who grew their hair into the shaggy pudding-basin cut the Fab Four favoured. Above all, the Beatles were in the money. Everything they touched turned to gold. Anything they endorsed sold. The pillow-cases they used in a hotel in Kansas City were cut into 160,000 1" squares, and sold for a dollar each.

Of course, America went overboard for the Beatles in its own special way. After years of home-grown musical fads this was something fresh and original. The Beatles, with their adenoidal Liverpool accents, sounded different, and they acted

differently too. They weren't the controlled 'image' most American performers presented. In the best British tradition they were disciplined but eccentric and on their first American trip, in February 1964, they gave one of the most irreverent press conferences since Groucho Marx. When asked: 'What about the movement in Detroit to stamp out Beatles?' The lads replied: 'We have a campaign to stamp out Detroit'.

British Meant Best

Meanwhile, surrounding Kennedy Airport were 10,000 teenagers who had already taken them to their hearts, chanting 'We love you Beatles, Oh yes we do'. It was the start of a British invasion, a time when British meant the best. Soon British groups, British actors, British models and designers, were making it mostly on the strength of the right accent and the right birthplace. Today the Beatles; tomorrow Quant, Twiggy, the Stones and Michael Caine.

Both in the States and Britain the whole point of the group seemed somehow lost amidst the acclaim. Basically the Beatles started out to make music as well as money; and although their records sold astronomically and they performed widely on stage and TV, the real cult was based on personality, not music. The first singles, 'Love Me Do' in October 1962, and 'Please Please Me' in January 1963, set the style of the early Beatles. The tunes

21

were catchy and melodic, and the lyrics banal; but either way their records were insufficient to account for Beatlemania. It wasn't until 'Rubber Soul' and the 'Revolver' album, that their music became wistful and witty and original; and this was because their success gave them the freedom to be more experimental and less directly commercial. Musically, the 'Beatle Years' left a fine heritage of humable standards. Lennon and McCartney were the new Cole Porter: 'Girl', 'Michelle' and 'And I Love Her' became classics that still sound good treated any way. Probably the lasting effect of Beatlemania on music today is not the records they left but the standard they bequeathed. Record stars had once been made on how they looked and how they sounded and the quality of their writers, and few could read or write music or play an instrument. The Beatles changed that, and now there are few chart-toppers who don't write and play as well as sing. Thousands of teenage boys went out to buy guitars and drum kits in the mid-'60s, and in the '70s they have become the nucleus of a pop world where talent and skill far outmatch opportunity.

Public Microscope

The people's millionaires though, finally grew tired of the people and turned their backs on them – and that was the beginning of the end. They started out simple and lovable, but they ended up outrageous. Knowing their every word and act was under the public microscope, the words and acts grew wilder as they searched for new experiences. John said the Beatles were more popular than Christ. Paul said he'd taken LSD. They

Right: A Beatle captured. Below: Recording manager George Martin.

got hooked on mysticism with the Maharishi. They did as they pleased because whatever they did the world still loved them, and gradually it pleased them to use their wealth for the most elusive luxury of all, privacy. Gradually Beatlemania faded as the four of them all in their different ways, withdrew from the spotlight and went about their own interests.

Probably the best explanation of the lengthy public fascination with the Beatles is that they were never static. It's natural to want what you can't have, and the Beatles steered a fine course between belonging to their public and to themselves. They gave plenty, but always retained a touch of unpredictability that no one could restrain. No one ever owned them, and just to prove it they always broke a few minor rules. And when one day it was over, towards the end of 1967, no one was any nearer to explaining what had caused the enormous excesses of

enthusiasm. The Beatles went on being popular, but the days when the stage would be buried under pounds of jelly babies, when the hospital where Ringo had his tonsils out had to issue *hourly* bulletins on his condition, the days of mass passion . . . were over.

George Martin, who produced their records, said of the Beatles: "They like everything to be like instant coffee. They want instant recording, instant films, instant everything." It was this that made them right for the fans bred in an instant culture, looking for an instant hero (or four). Martin also said: "They are very like children in many ways. They love anything magical" . . . which comes back to their very similarity to the millions for whom they became an obsession. We all take a childlike delight in impossible fantasy, and John, Paul, Ringo and George took the world on a magical mystery tour such as it is unlikely to ever see again.

The Beatles' US Tour '64 The Great Take-Over

With 'I Want To Hold Your Hand' topping the US singles charts and their first album rising fast, the Beatles hit America on a wave of publicity that was to swamp the world as 'the Liverpool Sound'.

'We want the Beatles, we want the Beatles' was the cry that drowned the noise of jet airliners at the John F. Kennedy International Airport one day in February, 1964, when John, Paul, George and Ringo touched down at the start of their first-ever American visit. Brian Epstein's dreams and expectations of the American response had come true. All the ballyhoo of the mass media was there to greet them, along with a screaming teenage crowd of 10,000.

The press conference, held at the airport, brought scenes of near hysteria as reporters, cameramen and photographers jostled and fought for the best positions. In the affray a well known DJ was threatened with violence by a TV newsman when he tried to get a personal interview with the boys — a threat transmitted throughout the American airwaves via the DJ's live microphone. Despite this, the conference was a great success. The Beatles had won the hearts of the American media and public with their sincere personalities, wit and charm, and the way they promptly and politely answered each question that was thrust upon them:

Q. ''Are you embarrassed by the Beatle-mania and near-lunacy that you create.''

John. ''No, it's great, we like lunatics, it's healthy.''

Q. ''Will you sing a song?''

All four. ''No.''

Q. ''Is it because you can't sing?''

John. ''No, we need money first.''

Q. ''How much money do you expect to take out of this country?''

John. ''About half-a-crown or two dollars.''

Q. ''Do you ever have haircuts?''

George. ''I had one yesterday.''

Ringo. ''It's no lie, you should have seen him the day before.''

Q. ''How do you account for your phenomenal success?''

John. ''If we knew, we would form another group and be managers.''

Q. ''Why do you sing like Americans and talk like Englishmen?''

John. ''It sells better.''

Q. ''Have you heard of the 'Stamp out the Beatles' campaign being organized by

a group of Detroit students, and exactly what do you intend to do about it?''

Paul. ''First of all we would bring out a 'Stamp out Detroit' campaign.''

Q. ''What do you think of Beethoven?''

Ringo. ''Great, especially his poems. I keep cracking that gag everyday.''

Q. ''Exactly when do you feel you will retire?''

George. ''When we get fed up with it, we're still enjoying it now, and we enjoyed it before we made any money.''

From the press conference at the airport they travelled in a virtual armed convoy to the Hotel Plaza in the centre of New York, where hundreds of teenage fans were waiting in the rain hoping to catch a glimpse of their new idols.

One of the prime reasons for their visit was an appearance on the famed *Ed Sullivan TV Show*. Again they were a massive success, and the show received its highest-ever ratings. While in New York, they also had some time for sightseeing, touring Greenwich Village in a hired limousine, twisting at the Peppermint Lounge, fooling with the Bunnies at Heffner's Playboy Club, and dining at the '21 Club'. Most of this socializing had been made

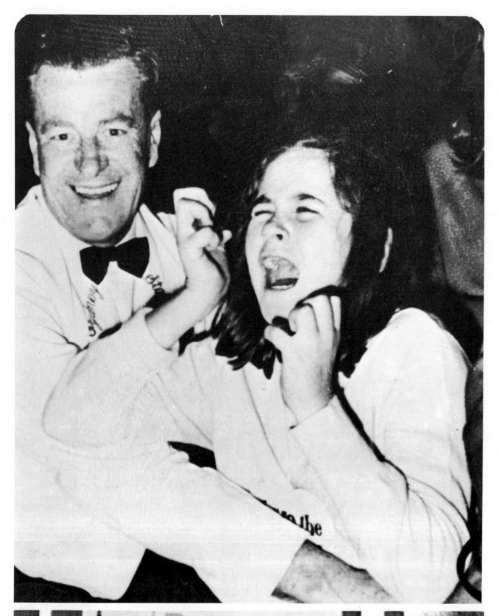

possible by Murray The K, the well-known New York DJ, who had arranged things with the clubs so that the Beatles could have a good time and get lots of newspaper coverage without all the harassments of having to meet the 'public' at every turn – George Harrison was even given the key to the New York Bunny Club.

The Beatles' first live performance in the States was due to be a one-night-stand at the Coliseum, a huge indoor stadium in Washington. They were due to fly down to Washington, but a snowstorm threatened so they cancelled the flight and travelled by train instead. Thousands and thousands of screaming fans were, predictably by now, waiting to mob them as the train pulled into Union Station, and hundreds of policemen were called in as the crowd surged forward bearing placards welcoming the Beatles to Washington.

The concert itself was a giant success, and the Fab Four played to a capacity crowd of 9,000 that behaved in much the same way as any British audience – so that the Beatles themselves couldn't be heard above the screaming, stamping mob. Someone backstage dutifully asked Paul how they could compete when the crowd got so noisy, and he replied: "When it gets so loud that they can't hear us, we usually take a rest and only mime the words without actually singing."

Having A Ball

As was fitting in those days of British export drives, Lord and Lady Ormsby-Gore, the British Ambassador and his wife, held a ball in honour of the boys at the British Embassy after their concert. During the evening Ringo was asked if he considered himself the sex-symbol of the group. He replied, with a laugh: "Look at me, you can see I'm no sex-symbol, you can see my face." His smile, though, quickly turned to anger when a socialite deb snipped at his hair with a pair of scissors. To fit in with the tone of the event, an Embassy spokesman was asked by one witty reporter if the Beatles were Britain's repayment for the Skybolt missile. "No," he said, "I think that they are Britain's way of paying America back for the many cans of Spam that were sent over during the war!"

After this performance the Beatles returned to New York for their next engagement at the famous Carnegie Hall. The two concerts there were solidly booked and thousands were turned away, but Mrs Nelson Rockefeller nevertheless attended one of the shows and let it be known just how wonderful she thought it all was. By the time John, Paul, George and Ringo had left the stage that night – bodies soaking in sweat, throats dry and hoarse – Beatlemania

Top left: The Beatles caused hysteria every time they appeared, whether in airport lounges or onstage. Left: Paul, John and Ringo appearing for newsmen with the New York skyline as a backdrop. George had tonsilitis at the time.

The Beatles played to capacity crowds at each venue. From the moment they appeared on stage the thousands of fans screamed their hearts out – often drowning the music of their idols.

Ed Sullivan congratulates the Beatles after their first appearance on American TV. Insert: A welcome break in Miami.

had without a doubt grafted its cancerous self onto teenage America.

To round off the visit the Beatles' last engagement was a re-appearance on the *Ed Sullivan Show*, this time to be televized from Miami Beach, Florida. When they flew into the Miami International Airport it was to the biggest welcome of the tour, and the screaming fans broke through barricades, smashed windows, broke down doors and demolished chairs in their path. A large police escort helped the Beatles to their limousines, and saw them safely on their way to the Deauville Hotel. Behind them they left complete pandemonium, many teenage casualties and an airport that looked as though a siege had taken place.

The *Ed Sullivan Show* also heralded scenes of wild hysteria, for some reason more tickets had been issued than there were seats, and after queueing for a long time many disappointed kids were turned away. Some of them, from the University of Miami, later joined forces with a few Tamla Motown fans who had flown down from Detroit to continue their 'Stamp out the Beatles' campaign. As a result, police were called in to quell a demonstration outside the Beatles' hotel, and the inevitable clashes between this angered minority group and the majority of pro-Beatle fans. The lucky ones, however, who did manage to get a seat at the show, had a marvellous time.

During the last few days of their tour the Beatles had a holiday, and spent their time either in a private swimming pool or sunbathing on a borrowed yacht. When they weren't doing this they were messing about on motor-boats, chatting up girls at the Miami Beach Peppermint Lounge and The Wreck Bar in the Castaways Motel. The police sergeant who was in charge of their security during their stay in Miami even invited the boys to dinner with his family – they accepted – and experienced for the first time real American home-cooking.

Finally, though, they returned to New York, and after a short stop for another press conference left for Britain victorious. They returned to the States in the August of that year for their first extensive tour, which took in 24 cities with 31 performances. They returned also in 1965 and 1966, playing New York's Shea Stadium both times to capacity crowds of true believers. Their last live performance anywhere in the world was in San Francisco on August 29th, 1966, but in many ways what had made it all possible was the inspired handling of that first US visit, and the cheery, family appeal they managed to present so well to so many different kinds of people.

The Fab Four appearing again for the newsmen – this time in Washington.

Popperfoto

27

The Music of The Beatles

When Paul McCartney and John Lennon entered the recording business in October 1962, they were to make innovations which eleven years later, became standard practice. Besides changing the entire face of pop music, they also introduced the singer/songwriter syndrome which has now become as commonplace as the group itself.

When Paul and John wrote and recorded 'Love Me Do' and 'P.S. I Love You' the common practice at that time was for a group's manager to scout the offices of Denmark Street, London's Tin Pan Alley, to see if he could find suitable material for his artists. Having found a song which he considered suitable, he would present it to the group and upon their approval (although groups or singers in the early '60s had very little say in what they did) they would record it. The composer of the song would receive his royalty and go away happy. He hadn't written the song for anybody in particular, so the fact that someone had come along, picked up on his song and made a successful record from it was his good fortune.

Four Young Novices

Paul and John changed all this. They believed, quite rightly, that if they wrote the material they were to record, not only would they pick up a greater percentage of the royalty, but they could adapt the song, through the Beatles, to how they had written it to be performed. Of course, the hierarchy would have to approve of this 'unorthodox' policy — after all, having just received a hard-earned contract, they could hardly start dictating to the higher echelons of EMI. They suggested the idea to George Martin, their newly acquired recording manager, and in Martin's own words: "I was convinced that I had a hit

group on my hands if only I could get hold of the right songs." One assumed he meant somebody else's. He searched for the right song but couldn't find anything to surpass 'Love Me Do', so he reluctantly released it as their first single.

What George Martin didn't know when he made his first reluctant decision was that, by letting these four young novices have their own way, he was revolutionising the shape of things to come; for in a matter of a few years a group would find it unthinkable to record other writers' material all the time.

It would be extremely difficult to pinpoint Paul and John's influences as far as their writing is concerned. Certainly we know that Tamla Motown, rock & roll and rhythm & blues were influencing them as a group. One has only to listen to some of their early repertoire to know that Little Richard was highly respected as far as the boys were concerned. It is interesting to compare any of Little Richard's songs with the McCartney rocker 'I'm Down', and the fact that three of their first four albums ('Hard Day's Night' being the exception) contained songs by influential writers, indicated that they were still to find their own direction.

But why did they record other people's songs? Well, it could have been for one of two main reasons. Firstly, they hadn't yet written enough songs, or songs of high enough quality to fill an album containing 12 tracks — although this seems highly unlikely since they still wrote prolifically whilst they were on tour. On the other hand they could genuinely have wanted to record the songs of the people who were giving them a guiding light.

The Motown Influence

If we look at the songs that the Beatles recorded by other writers on their earlier albums what do we find? 'Twist And Shout', 'Money', 'Please Mr. Postman', 'Devil In Her Heart' and 'You Really Got A Hold On Me' were all from Berry Gordy's

Oriole stable (later to be re-named Tamla Motown). Their interest in this music was a good four years ahead of most of the record buying public. Indeed it was the Beatles themselves who introduced most people to Tamla in a big way. Who knew that the Isley Brothers recorded 'Twist And Shout', and that Barrett Strong's 'Money' was the first ever Motown release? Taking a closer look at their repertoire would also show how two 'show' songs were included: 'Till There Was You' and 'A Taste Of Honey'. It would seem that Paul had an interest in these purely from a writing point of view. Was the style of these types of song the warm-up to such great McCartney ballads as 'Michelle', 'And I Love Her' and 'Yesterday', to name but three? It seems a strange coincidence that it was Paul who sang these obviously out-of-place songs in an act that was so strongly rock orientated.

Next we have, of course, rock & roll. Chuck Berry, Carl Perkins, Buddy Holly and Little Richard songs were all featured on three of their early albums, and the boys never disguised the fact that these performers had a great influence on the

Syndication International

And Shout', the Beatles proceeded to scale the heights of popular taste. They came to represent the peak of pop writing, and found themselves able to restrict their records and repertoire to original material only. During this undisputed reign of commercial Beatle pop, the albums 'Hard Day's Night', 'With The Beatles', 'Help' and 'Rubber Soul' presented their music as the most desirable and successful brand of pop ever to emerge from Britain.

This period can perhaps be looked back on as the Beatles' mainstream. They were copied and covered by hoardes of other artists. But the sort of music that the world took to be the Beatles best was a collection of those songs which most supported the public's conception of the group: a middle ground of Lennon and McCartneyism. With the Beatles busy touring and filming, as well as making records, and with Beatle wigs and clothes being marketed all over the world, they were big business. Lennon and McCartney were each developing their own approach to music, but because the Beatles were being offered to the world almost as Siamese quads, four lovable cheeky heads on one money-making body, the songs that were the hit singles were carefully selected mainstream tunes. Paul's 'She's A Woman', or John's 'You Can't Do That' may have been commercial, but they didn't project the one-ness of the group as well as 'I Feel Fine' or 'Help' — with their characteristic join-in vocals and off-beat drumming that distinguished so much of the Beatles' mainstream pop.

In this period, of course, the hit single was still the touchstone of pop success. The group's album sales were crucial in turning the pop world on to the money that could be made out of LPs, but it was through singles that a group's desired image was projected. 'I Feel Fine', 'Ticket To Ride', 'Paperback Writer', 'Help' and 'Hard Day's Night' were all 'Lennon-and-McCartney' songs, rather than being identified with one or other of the two writers. The albums, too, carried mainstream songs, 'Drive My Car' and 'Eight Days A Week' for example, and these songs all succeeded because they contained elements of both Lennon's and McCartney's style. But there was always space on the albums for more characteristic songs as well. 'Yesterday' from Paul, and 'Norwegian Wood' from John, were indications that the Beatles' success was not merely based on a chance coming together of two ordinary writers to make great songs together. Instead, notice was served that here were two different and very considerable talents who wrote together sometimes, but who would be able to compose fine songs on their own, too.

John Lennon's Music: 1962—66.

Lennon's own music is less easily categorised than McCartney's. Lennon has his different moods, but these are not as distinct as McCartney's rock style and ballad style. Because John Lennon's songs seem more personal and less 'composed' than many of McCartney's, the different styles of writing merge into a music which is definable only as 'Lennon's'. His music was born out of his time, his experiences and observations, rather than being influenced by traditional songwriting approaches. His songs, especially in the early years, were personal because they related to the 'boy and girl' problems of those who bought the records. His approach was more earthy and English, but at the same time his early musical ideas were not particularly profound.

Lennon's ballad style is a recognisable one, for he wrote far more slow and melodic songs than one might assume. 'If I Fell', 'This Boy', 'It's Only Love', 'Girl' and 'In My Life' all project Lennon into the middle of his songs. But 'If I Fell' for example, is as tuneful as many of McCartney's ballads. Unlike McCartney, Lennon didn't write much straightforward rock & roll. Though influenced, as Paul was, by Chuck Berry, Little Richard, and other contemporary black American artists, the influences tend to show in harmonica-tinged, bluesy approaches. On the earliest records songs like 'Thank You Girl', 'You Can't Do That', 'Love Me Do', and 'I Should Have Known Better' show how Lennon merged his influences into his roots to produce a style that, while based on the music he listened to, was very personal to him. McCartney, on the other hand, was more likely to come up with a straight, gutsy number like 'I'm Down', directly influenced by Little Richard's 'Long Tall Sally'.

Many of Lennon's songs can't be defined in terms of style, perhaps because of the way in which he has often adapted his influences so much. His wry humour shows through in 'Norwegian Wood'; while in 'Nowhere Man' — one of the few Lennon songs in which he doesn't write about himself — Lennon offers a strong melodic ballad, but with a slow, country blues rhythm, and typical Lennon lyrics. The early Lennon compositions were you and me songs; they are real because they are about such limited and identifiable subjects. It was only slowly, therefore, that Lennon's experiences as a member of the Beatles seemed to take their place in his lyrics.

Paul McCartney's Music: 1962—66

'All My Loving' was the first hint that Paul did in fact write songs on his own, and although for many this wasn't obvious it became clearly apparent in albums to follow. As was said earlier, McCartney's songs fell into two definable categories, one being ballads and the other being rock in the true sense of the word. Of course there was the 'mainstream', but that has been dealt with already.

McCartney showed his liking for slow bally material on the first album when he sang 'A Taste Of Honey', and continued on the next album with 'Till There Was You'; but both of these songs were non-original. McCartney was to change this, so much so that to think of Beatle ballads now means thinking of Paul McCartney. The first traces

shape the Beatles were to take. In fact as early as 1962, shortly after the release of 'Love Me Do', George Harrison openly announced that the four above-mentioned, plus the Everly Brothers, had a great deal to do with the way in which the Beatles music was being directed. Much later, in 1965, one song featured on the album and in the film 'Help', 'You've Got To Hide Your Love Away', had such obvious Dylan influences that it brought the American even more to the fore than he was already.

So there's no doubt that the Beatles, just like anyone else, had their influences. The peculiar thing is that the people who influenced them as writers and performers eventually finished up being influenced by them. An example of this was the album released from the Motown stable entitled 'Motown Sings Lennon And McCartney'. But who wasn't to sing Lennon and McCartney?

With the emergence of 'Hard Day's Night', — a film, an album, and a single sharing the same title, — the Beatles' music seemed to change gear. From the early period, when their obvious influences led them to record, for example, 'Twist

of his ability to write such profound melodies appeared on the album 'Hard Day's Night', when he came up with two songs which since have been covered widely: 'And I Love Her' and 'Things We Said Today'. His rock writing wasn't being neglected however, and on the same album he wrote such a good rocker that it was eventually released as a single: 'Can't Buy Me Love'.

Although not a lot came from McCartney on their next album, 'Beatles For Sale', it was 'Help' that made it clear how this young Liverpudlian could develop along the lines of your Cole Porters, Hoagy Carmichaels and George Gershwins. 'I've Just Seen A Face', 'The Night Before' and 'Another Girl' were all good meaty rock songs containing slight tinges of 'mainstream'. It was, however, the only ballad that he wrote for that album, a song which didn't even appear in the film, that caused the greatest sensation. 'Yesterday' was a sympathetic ballad, beautifully arranged for a string quartet with only McCartney singing or playing. In many ways this was a complete McCartney composition, and for the first time the world was made to realise that Paul and John did, in fact, write separately. 'Yesterday' left such an impact in the world of pop music that it has since become the most-covered Beatle song.

As if 'Yesterday' wasn't good enough, McCartney did it yet again with another ballad entitled 'Michelle'. A song very much in the same vein as 'Yesterday', this was equally as popular. It was at this time, with all due respect to Lennon, that people were dubbing McCartney as 'the real writer', the man that was able to compose the standards. Again, on the next album 'Revolver', McCartney proved to the world that here was the best composer Britain had produced for many a decade. When people first heard 'Eleanor Rigby' they were shouting McCartney's praises the world over. After all he had now written three world-class ballads on three consecutive albums – not a bad track record!

A Rock Writer

Despite the ingenious talent Paul had for writing memorable ballads, he never flagged as a rock writer. 'She's A Woman', 'Day Tripper', 'I'm Down', 'Drive My Car' and 'Got To Get You Into My Life' were all songs that could well have been written and recorded in the late '50s or pre-Beatle '60s. The latter song was very soul-tinged, and at the time it wouldn't have been surprising if a soul artist from the Stax stable had picked up on it.

'Revolver' was McCartney's most prolific album in terms of composing. On this he wrote, as well as 'Eleanor Rigby', two ballads of equal class: 'For No One' and 'Here There And Everywhere'; and 'Good Day Sunshine' could well have made it as a single. There was no longer any doubt over his ability as a tunesmith supreme, but he was hardly as personal as Lennon. Many of McCartney's lyrics were written in the third person, he wrote out of his

head rather than through his eyes. 'Eleanor Rigby', 'Michelle', 'For No One' and 'Here There And Everywhere' were all, or so it seems, figments of Paul's imagination. A perfectly well-balanced contrast to the first person songs of John Lennon.

McCartney had hit on a formula that proved so successful he felt he really didn't need to change it. Lennon, on the other hand, was continually changing, looking for something new, wanting to play with sounds. The second period of the Beatles was to confirm that statement beyond all doubt.

Musical Maturity

'Revolver' was an overdue album. Off the road at last, the Beatles had a lot of resting to do before they were ready to set about recording. And although in retrospect 'Rubber Soul' seems to have hinted at increasing musical maturity, in 1965 it was just another Beatle album. It sold and sold of course – but then all Beatle LPs did. Nonetheless, some people felt that with the touring over, the Beatles' light would begin to wane.

Brian Epstein might have felt this too. Certainly he felt that he had less real influence over the group than in the early days. But far from deteriorating, the music of Lennon and McCartney became stronger and more sophisticated. When 'Revolver' was released, in summer 1966, it had a lot of people reconsidering their opinion of Lennon and McCartney. Were they just clever compilers of catchy choruses, or did they have deeper and more timeless talents?

'Revolver' suggested that the two writers were progressing along divergent paths. Although hardly ever writing together, they were still able to use recording sessions and other meetings to comment on each other's work, and to test the quality of their writing against each others criticism. McCartney developed through his ballads, with the tasteful orchestrations that were one of George Martin's important contributions to the Beatles' work.

Lennon's music was also growing. With 'I'm Only Sleeping', 'She Said She Said', and 'Doctor Robert', his dry sceptical lyrics were well-married to some atmospheric and melodic tunes. 'And Your Bird Can Sing' was again John Lennon, and showed that his work was becoming more polished without losing any of its bite. Following 'Revolver' a new and more lasting respect was accorded McCartney and Lennon by many critics.

Drug Influence

Of course, all the songs were still 'Beatle' songs, not least because that's how everyone wanted them to be. But the massive commercial pressure to conform to the image the public cherished – especially in the days of touring had started to ease. By then the difference between Lennon's and McCartney's music had become increasingly apparent. 'Good

PENNY LANE

Penny Lane: there is a barber
taking photographs
Of every head he's had the pleasure to know
And all the people that come and go
Stop and say hello.

On the corner is a banker with a motor car.
The little children laugh at him
behind his back.
And the banker never wears a mac
In the pouring rain,
Very strange!

Penny Lane is in my ears and in my eyes,
Wet beneath the blue suburban skies,
I sit and meanwhile, back in Penny Lane:
There is a fireman with an hour-glass
And in his pocket is a portrait of the Queen,
He likes to keep his fire engine clean,
It's a clean machine.

Penny Lane is in my ears and in my eyes,
Full of fish-and-finger pies
In summer, meanwhile, back
behind the shelter
In the middle of the round-about
A pretty nurse is selling poppies from a tray,
And though she feels she's in a play
She is anyway.

Penny Lane: the barber shaves
another customer
We see the banker sitting, waiting for a trim
And then the fireman rushes in
From the pouring rain
Very strange!

PENNY LANE .... *by Lennon & McCartney.*
© *Dick James Music Ltd.*

PLEASE PLEASE ME

Last night I said these words to my girl,
'I know you never even try, girl.
Come on, come on, come on, come on
Please please me, oh yeah,
Like I please you.'

You don't need me to show the way, love
Why do I always have to say, love,
Come on, come on, come on, come on,
Please please me, oh yeah,
Like I please you.

I don't want to sound complaining
But you know there's always rain in
My heart.
In my heart.
I do all the pleasing with you
It's so hard to reason with you
Oh yeah
Why do you make me blue?

Last night I said these words to my girl
'I know you never even try girl
Come on, come on, come on, come on.
Please please me, oh yeah,
Like I please you.
Me, oh yeah, like I please you
Me, oh yeah, like I please you.'

PLEASE PLEASE ME ...... *by Lennon & McCartney.*
© *1967. Used by permission of Northern Songs.*

Day Sunshine' is the only track which harks back to the 'mainstream'. But signposts of future development were also there. George Harrison had always been 'allowed' a track or two on previous albums, but they had never been highly rated, even by the other Beatles — though 'If I Needed Someone', for example, had clearly shown that he had songwriting talent.

But on 'Revolver', George, with 'Taxman' and 'I Want To Tell You', first gave real notice of his late-flowering talents. The influence of Indian music, as on his 'Love You Too', was perhaps to be as liberating as the bright talents of McCartney and Lennon had been over-powering. And, of course, the group's interests in drugs, which were to influence their next album 'Sgt Pepper' as well as the whole youth movement, were most clearly presaged in Lennon's 'Tomorrow Never Knows'.

It was probably firstly on 'Revolver' that the different songwriting approaches of Lennon and McCartney, the tense imagery of John, and Paul's dramatic storytelling—were beginning to show themselves. And then along came 'Sgt. Pepper', and the rock world had found itself an undisputed standard.

Paul had originally written a good rocker, 'Sgt. Pepper's Lonely Hearts Club Band', and had an idea to build an album around the song. As with so many albums before,

John and Paul started tinkling their pianos, strumming their guitars, scanning the newspapers and watching TV in a search for inspiration. With some help from their friends – a word here, a phrase there – they had Ringo's song in the bag.

John based his song 'Good Morning, Good Morning' on a Kelloggs Cornflakes TV commercial; while his 'Lucy In The Sky With Diamonds' was inspired by a painting that his son, Julian brought home from school one day (it had the added advantage of throwing the US rock press into disarray when they realised the initials were LSD!); and Paul's 'She's Leaving Home' came from a *Daily Mirror* story. Also from a newspaper story came the last verse of 'A Day In The Life', mainly written by John, but with Paul supplying the middle dream sequence.

Probably one of the best songs in this era missed a place on the album. 'Across The Universe' was Lennon at his best, and the words flow into each other as one line flows into the next:

'Words are flying out like endless rain into
  a paper cup
They slither while, they pass, they slip
  away across the universe'

The song was given away to the World Wildlife Fund, and sank into the obscurity of a 'Various Artists' compilation; to be resurrected, re-recorded and released on

'Let It Be' — only time and production having taken some of its magic away.

'Penny Lane'/'Strawberry Fields Forever' was issued before the album, and had already taken the public by surprise. In the days when Beatles singles went straight to the no. 1 slot, it had seemed they were on the wane as the single just hung around the no. 2 position. Although their last two singles, 'Paperback Writer' and 'Eleanor Rigby', were also untypical, the boy/girl situation was still expected by the fans. John based his song around the reality/unreality situation of a mental institution outside Liverpool. 'Strawberry Fields Forever' was, however, full of Lennon's experimental ideas, and clearly bore the signs of LSD experience in the jocular nihilism of its lyrics:

'Let me take you down,
'Cos I'm going to Strawberry Fields
Nothing is real
And nothing to get hung about'

In contrast to John's writing, Paul's bouncy, melodic story in 'Penny Lane' — a song typical of nearly all his ballads since 1963 — described an everyday Liverpool street in almost fairy tale terms. This trend in Paul's work was to continue through 'Sgt. Pepper', and later enabled him to conceive the idea of 'Magical Mystery Tour'. The single, however, finally became a milestone along with 'Sgt. Pepper', an

album that to many people the Beatles have never equalled or surpassed. From that time on, other groups' best works have usually been tagged 'their 'Sgt. Pepper''.

The film of *Magical Mystery Tour* took the public by surprise when it was screened in Britain by the BBC on Boxing Day 1967. It wasn't exactly the holiday entertainment people were used to, and didn't ever rate as a star-studded spectacular — it was just a simple, original, sometimes beautiful short film. There had already been a preview of the music on the 'B' side of 'Hello Goodbye' in the form of John's 'I Am The Walrus' — the first Beatles song to incorporate Hari Krishna in its lyrics. 'Walrus' was probably the highlight of John's intense imagery songs:

'Yellow matter custard dripping from a
*   dead dog's eye*
Crabalocker fishwife pornographic priestess
Boy you been a naughty girl,
You let your knickers down.'

Although many of the songs on 'Magical Mystery Tour' weren't of the same quality as those on 'Sgt. Pepper', 'I Am The Walrus' and 'The Fool On The Hill' still contained the magic. 'Fool On The Hill' was a continuation of Paul's romantic melodic theme; a natural progression from 'Yesterday', 'Michelle', 'Here There And Everywhere' and 'She's Leaving Home'.

Another noteworthy song on the album — showing Paul's continuing interest in the 1930's that had been there since the Cavern days and numbers like 'When I'm Sixty-Four' — came out again on this album with 'Your Mother Should Know', on which he captured that same nostalgic mood beautifully.

While the Beatles were in India in 1968 holidaying with the Maharishi, John and Paul wrote many new songs. When they returned there were strong rumours of a new album titled 'Get Back', with songs like 'Teddy Boy', 'Junk' and the title song; even the cover was announced as having the Beatles standing on the steps of the EMI building — as on their first album, 'Please Please Me', and their 1973 greatest hits set. What they *did* produce was 'The Beatles', a mixed helping of rock that showed a swing away from lush production towards a more uncomplicated, earthy rock & roll.

'Baby You're A Rich Man'

Also released at this time was the soundtrack from the full-length cartoon feature *Yellow Submarine* — not really a stunning new album, especially as what was probably the best song written for the film, 'Baby You're A Rich Man', had already been put out as the 'B' side of 'All You Need Is Love'. The Beatles' 'White' album that came at the end of 1968 nevertheless covered all the streams of their writing.

From the straight rock & roll of 'Back In The USSR' (a mixture of Berry and the Beach Boys) and 'Birthday'; to the romantic 'Mother Nature's Son', 'I Will' and 'Julia'; the story-in-a-song of 'Rocky Racoon', 'Bungalow Bill' and 'Ob-La-Di, Ob-La-Da'; and the strong images of 'Glass Onion', 'Cry Baby Cry' and 'Happiness Is A Warm Gun', the album represented as wide a range of material as anything the Beatles had offered up before.

Also in 1968, in the midst of the British rock & roll nostalgia revival, had come Paul's Presley-esque 'Lady Madonna', and what was probably *the* song of 1968 — or even the '60s — Paul's gigantic 'Hey Jude', backed with John's 'Revolution'. They had done it again; as during their whole career it had seemed that when the Beatles' talent was wearing thin they stood up and showed the world where their music was at.

But it wasn't long before disillusion started to set in. John's interests outside the Beatles were becoming more important to him, and his avant-garde music with Yoko Ono and the Plastic Ono Band was taking most of his time. It was left to Paul to keep the Beatles Myth alive. In the midst of apathy and eternal business troubles at Apple he organised the *Let It Be* film, and up there on the big screen the world witnessed the end. What music there was, was very thin — apart from John's revamped 'Across The Universe'. The songs were by now mainly left in Paul's hands. He produced the gospel-flavoured title song 'Let It Be', the rocking 'Get Back', and his hopefully romantic 'Long And Winding Road'.

John's lack of fresh material was sadly missed, but he had nevertheless been quite

successful with his Plastic Ono Band singles 'Give Peace A Chance', 'Cold Turkey' and 'Instant Karma' — with a chord sequence borrowed from 'All You Need Is Love'. Also released under the Beatles label at this time was the magnificent 'The Ballad Of John And Yoko', recorded by just John and Paul with John supplying the Berry-type lead guitar lick, and Paul on bass and drums.

It seemed a difficult period for the foundering career of the Beatles, but they somehow managed to keep the Myth alive with the last album they were to record together (although it was released before 'Let It Be'), 'Abbey Road'. The 'Let It Be' recordings were just left lying around because, for the first time since 'Please Please Me', no one wanted anything to do with their material. Eventually the tapes were handed over to Glyn Johns to try and make an album.

Although 'Abbey Road' may have kept the Myth alive through 1969, and could be called 'Sgt. Pepper Part Two', it was dismal to realize that the Beatles had got to a point where Paul was too embarrassed to ask John if he could sing harmony on John's 'Come Together'. 'Come Together', though, found John at his strongest, and firmly in the 'Walrus' vein with the best song he'd produced for some months.

John's 'I Want You (She's So Heavy)' on 'Abbey Road' was, however, not quite as successful — based as it was on an R&B structure similar to Bob Dorough and Ben Tucker's 'Comin' Home Babe'. The 15-minute sequence of 'Sun King', 'Mean Mr. Mustard' and 'Polythene Pam' stood out on side two of the album as unquestionably John's contribution, as did his other interesting song on the album, 'Because', which was written with the help of Yoko and Beethoven's 'Moonlight Sonata'.

Final Session

Paul also supplied a varied assortment of songs for 'Abbey Road'. 'Maxwell's Silver Hammer', which had first been introduced being rehearsed in the film *Let It Be*, was a typical McCartney story-in-a-song. For his second contribution, a rocker called 'Oh! Darling', Paul had arrived early at the studio every day for a week to sing it to himself and so make his voice hoarse as though he'd been performing on stage for a week. He also made up the majority of a 15-minute sequence with his beautiful 'You Never Give Me Your Money', 'Golden Slumbers', and the good-time rocker, 'She Came In Through The Bathroom Window'. The sequence, made up mostly of material John and Paul had written while in India, wasn't completed as individual songs, but nevertheless formed an interesting collage. The closing of the album, and ironically the Beatles' career together, was marked by Paul's karmic song, 'The End'.

'And in the end the love you take is equal
*   to the love you make'*

George Harrison's first credit as a song-writer had been for an instrumental written with John Lennon and recorded in the early

Top left: Ringo, the Beatle who remained almost untouched by it all. Top right: Singing 'Get Back' on the roof of Apple in London during the filming of *Let It Be*. **Bottom left: George and Pattie Boyd with the Maharishi. Bottom right: A late publicity shot.**

days in Hamburg. Then there was a gap until the Beatles' second album 'With The Beatles', and the song 'Don't Bother Me'. Then a further gap until 'Help', with 'I Need You' and 'You Like Me Too Much'. 'If I Needed Someone' from 'Rubber Soul' was, however, the first song to put George in the Lennon/McCartney class; this was his first song to be covered by another artist (the Hollies), and become a hit.

Then came 'Revolver' and George's opening track 'Taxman'. Here was a typical Beatles opener in the same vein as Lennon and McCartney's 'Rubber Soul' opener 'Drive My Car' – a good solid beat with a nice catch-phrase. The Indian influenced 'Love You Too' wasn't the first time George had played sitar on record – he had already used the instrument on John's 'Norwegian Wood' – but this time he was joined by Anil Bhagwat on tabla.

'Sgt. Pepper' brought Indian influence to the ears of the public in a big way with 'Within You Without You', and from this point on George really started experimenting. 'Blue Jay Way' from 'Magical Mystery Tour' was the result, and found him using images almost as well as Lennon.

George contributed two songs on the *Yellow Submarine* soundtrack, 'Only A Northern Song' and 'It's All Too Much', in which he incorporates some beautiful feedback at the start, and a couple of lines

from an old Merseybeats' hit 'Sorrow', in the final fade. He was writing so much in those days that John at one point remarked: "George is turning out songs like soft Mick these days."

George in fact was digesting influences from all around him – the Band, Bob Dylan, Lennon and McCartney, India, the Blues – everything and everyone. The 'B' sides of Beatles singles were by now becoming an outlet for George's writing skill and 'The Inner Light', the 'B' side of 'Lady Madonna', drew fine compliments from Paul: "Forget the Indian music and listen to the melody. Don't you think it's a beautiful melody? It's really lovely."

The 'White' album again showed George had the wit and imagery of John in songs like 'Piggies' and 'While My Guitar Gently Weeps', which incorporated Eric Clapton playing lead guitar. 'Something' from 'Abbey Road', could even have been pure Paul McCartney despite the suggestion that the opening line had come from a song James Taylor had recorded on Apple a year before titled 'Something In The Way She Moves'.

The question of originality, in fact, seemed to plague George's writing. It arose again later with 'My Sweet Lord', which closely resembled the Chiffons' 'He's So Fine'; but there can be no question as to the Harrison song on the 'Abbey

Road' album – 'Here Comes The Sun' was beautifully inspired. In retrospect it's a shame to think of how George had already penned 'All Things Must Pass' at the time of 'Let It Be', as had Paul with 'Teddy Boy' and 'Junk' from his first solo album.

Although 'All Things Must Pass' was written at the time of 'Let It Be', George's contributions to that album were in no way as innovative; the waltz tempo 'I Me Mine', and the straight 12-bar blues 'For You Blue' were both, however, proof of a fine songwriting talent.

Ringo's songwriting career started when he was credited along with Lennon and McCartney for the C&W flavoured 'What Goes On' on 'Rubber Soul'. Then came another rocka-hillbilly, 'Don't Pass Me By', from the 'White' album, and a glimpse of Ringo and George rehearsing 'Octopus's Garden' on the set of the *Let It Be* film – a recording later released on 'Abbey Road'. Ringo has often admitted that he only knows three chords, but he certainly makes the most of them, and with his LPs and singles of the '70s appears to be enjoying the musical possibilities of life outside the old foursome.

Since the demise of the Beatles in 1970 all four have had successful albums and written good-quality songs, but somehow the magic of a new Beatles album has yet to be captured.

34

The Beatle-Maker

On thinking back to the Beatles' beginnings, or come to that the beginnings of British pop music, a name that inevitably springs to mind is that of Brian Epstein. It was he who was without any doubt the finest manipulator of groups either before, during, or since the rise of the Beatles. His untimely death occurred in August 1967, and in many ways from that point on the Beatles started a slow downhill slide.

Brian was born on September 19th, 1934, in Rodney Street, Liverpool — an exclusive area well known for its concentration of doctors. The grandson of a Polish immigrant, Brian was the first of two children born to Queenie and Harry Epstein. At the age of four he attended kindergarten, which seems to have been one of the very few, if not only, schools that he ever came to terms with. When the war broke out Liverpool became a prime bombing target because of the docks, and along with hundreds of other children, Brian was evacuated to Southport, a West Coast resort now better known for convalescing. He was sent to Southport College where he carried on, after a fashion, his schooling.

In 1943 the bombing seemed to have stopped, and the Epstein family returned to Childwall, a suburb of Liverpool. Obviously the move meant Brian would have to leave Southport College, and after an interview with the headmaster of Liverpool College he was admitted as a scholar. His stay was not a very long or rewarding one for after a short period he was expelled. Brian once said: "One feature of life which I experienced there and at other schools and even sometimes now, was anti-semitism. Even now it lurks around the corner in some guise or other, and though it doesn't matter to me any more, it did when I was younger."

Harry Epstein was wondering whether his son and heir was ever going to find a school which he enjoyed, and the thought of having a totally un-educated son was worrying both him and his wife. Between them they decided, as a result of Brian's anti-semitic claims, to send him to a Jewish prep school, 'Beaconsfield', near Tunbridge Wells in Kent. Brian stayed at this prep school for the longest period of time that he stayed at any school, and when he was approaching the age of 13 he sat the examinations that would determine whether he would go forward to public school. Needless to say, the outcome was . . . failure.

To say that at this time Harry and Queenie were immensely worried about their son's future would be a gross understatement. However, they found a private school for their son in Dorset. At this school, if nothing else, he was allowed to express his flair for art, and remembers it as being the only thing that he was remotely good at. Back in Liverpool at this

time, Harry Epstein was trying hard to find a good school for Brian before it was too late. His hard work bore fruit, for in the autumn of 1948, just as Brian had turned 14, he was notified that his son was to attend Wrekin College in Shropshire.

At Wrekin, Brian discovered that he had another talent besides art. He took part in school plays and found that his performances were being praised by the teachers. It must have been the only thing young Epstein was praised for, and before he had the opportunity to sit any examinations he decided he wanted to leave school and become a dress designer. Brian might have *wanted* to become a dress designer but his parents had other ideas, and on September 10th, 1950, aged very nearly 16, he started his first job as a sales assistant at the family's local furniture store.

He started work at £5 a week, which really wasn't a bad wage at that time, and slowly but surely built up some kind of interest in his work. His parents were pleased as this was the first time in his life that he had shown concern for anything. Mr. and Mrs. Epstein were satisfied and happy with their eldest son. Things were on the up and up for Brian.

On December 9th, 1952, as though he hadn't gone through enough discipline of one sort or another, a buff envelope arrived through the door notifying him that he was to attend a National Service medical. (In those days National Service was compulsory). He passed his medical as an A.1., the only A.1. achievement he had ever received. And so he began his two years' service as a clerk in the Royal Army Service Corps.

Secure Businessman

Within 10 months of joining the army his nerves became seriously upset. He reported to the barrack doctor, and after a thorough examination he was passed on to a psychiatrist. After four psychiatric opinions they came to the conclusion that Private Epstein was just not fit for military service – and discharged him.

He arrived back in Liverpool prepared to work very hard at the furniture trade. This he did, and seemed to settle into some kind of routine way of life. His parents were happy. For no apparent reason at this time Brian's old love for acting returned, and he regularly attended the Liverpool Playhouse. He began to meet the actors socially, and started toying with the idea of acting as a profession. With the encouragement of the professionals Brian got himself an audition at the Royal Academy of Dramatic Arts, and after reading two pieces, excerpts from 'Confidential Clerk' and 'Macbeth', he was accepted to begin studies as from the next term. So at 22, although a secure and aspiring businessman, he submitted himself once again to the rigours of community life, and became a student at R.A.D.A. It didn't take Brian too long to realise that studying just wasn't his forte, and he went back, once again, to the furniture business – where it now seemed that

he was going to spend the rest of his working life.

The Epstein's store was at this time expanding, and they opened another branch in the city centre. Included in this branch was a record department which Brian took charge of. Anne Shelton opened the store, and from that first day it began to flourish. Although most of the records Brian sold were pop, his real interest lay in classical and his favourite composer was Sibelius.

In 1959 the Epstein's opened yet another store, this time in the heart of Liverpool's shopping centre and opened by Anthony Newley. By autumn 1962 Brian's store, for he was in complete charge of the city centre branch, was running to absolute perfection.

The Beatles

At about 3 o'clock on Saturday October 28th, 1961, a young customer came into the store, dressed in the usual costume of the time – black leather jacket and denim jeans – he said: "There's a record I want. It's 'My Bonnie', and it was made in Germany. Have you got it?" Brian knew his stock inside out and gave a negative nod: but the old policy of keeping the customer satisfied was now to pay handsome dividends. "Who is it by?" asked Brian. "You won't have heard of them" said the young customer, "it's a group called the Beatles . . ." He learned that they had just returned from Hamburg, Germany, and were currently playing a residency at the local Cavern club.

Curiosity overtook Brian, and he decided to visit this cellar club and find out what it was about this group that made the locals react as they did.

He wasn't too impressed with what he heard, although he found their personalities

magnetic and for this reason he stayed until they completed their set. When they left the stage he was taken to the band room to meet them, but merely for the purpose of asking them about their record. George was the first to speak to him. He shook Brian by the hand and said: "What brings Mr. Epstein here?" They obviously knew of him from the record store. Brian went ahead and explained the situation about the several requests he had had for their record. George called over John, Paul and Pete Best – and said "this man would like to hear our disc". They played it to him, and on hearing it Brian asked the four young lads to visit his office a few days later. Their first meeting was set for December 3rd, 1961.

Brian, even if he was thinking about it, had as much idea of artist/management as he had about flying to the Moon, but something inside was burning to get these four scruffy kids under his ruling. The four of them arrived at his office as arranged, although Paul was a little late. They passingly discussed the future and contracts and then moved on to other topics of conversation. They drank a lot of coffee and arranged another meeting for the following Wednesday. In between time Brian paid a visit to the family solicitor, Rex Makin, to discuss what an artist/management contract consisted of. On asking him this question and then explaining the reasons for asking it, Makin added dryly, "oh, yes, another Epstein idea. How long before you lose interest in this one?"

Signed, Sealed And Settled

The second meeting took place as arranged, and with all members sitting in his rather plush office Brian said: "You need a manager, would you like me to do

Brian Epstein seen with John and George standing behind the bride at Ringo's wedding.

it?'' There was a pregnant silence, and then John looked up and said ''Yes.'' The others all agreed, and John again said: ''Right then Brian. Manage us, now. Where's the contract? I'll sign it.'' Brian had very little idea what a contract looked like, let alone could he produce one. But within a week Makin had drawn one up, and the following Wednesday it was ready for all to sign. John, Paul, George and Pete Best all put their signatures to the contract, and all were counter-signed by witness Alastair Taylor, Brian's assistant. The only signature that was always conspicuous by it's absence was that of Brian Epstein.

First Audition

Brian felt that the first task of a manager was to secure for his artists a recording contract. He managed to lure Mike Smith of Decca to the Cavern to see and hear the Beatles at work, and what Mr. Smith heard knocked him out. He went back to Decca and arranged for the four lads to attend an audition at the famous Decca Record Company. The boys plus Brian arrived in London on New Year's Eve 1961, and the following morning, with Brian at their sides, went to the recording studio for their first audition.

They played several numbers which were duly recorded, and having completed their task returned to Liverpool to await the voices from the hierarchy of Decca. In March 1962, three long months later, Brian was summoned to the Decca offices to meet Dick Rowe and Beecher Stevens, two important executives. On arrival he was shown into their suite of offices and asked to sit down. Dick Rowe was spokesman: ''Not to mince words Mr. Epstein, we don't like your boys' sound. Groups of guitarists are on the way out.'' Brian tried to hide his immense disappointment and replied: ''You must be out of your minds. These boys are going to explode. I am completely confident that one day they will be bigger than Elvis Presley.'' Dick Rowe was rather taken aback and, thinking it was Brian that was going out of his mind, said: ''The boys won't go, Mr. Epstein. We know these things. You have a good business in Liverpool. Stick to that!''

Thus ended the Decca saga. Brian, however, was determined that someone somewhere was going to like his Beatles. Pye, Philips, Columbia and countless others all rejected Brian's tapes. 'There's nothing there' they all said in their voices of authority.

As a final resort Brian was going to have an all-or-nothing raid on London. If nothing happened this time he would call it a day. He hadn't any idea where he was going to take the tapes, but he was determined to secure a contract. Through a string of coincidences Epstein met up with a gentleman named Syd Coleman, who was a music publisher looking for songs. Brian played him the boys' tapes and Coleman liked what he heard. He would, however, like a gentleman called George Martin to hear them, and would

Brian take them along to a company called Parlophone (part of the EMI group) and play them to him? This Brian did, and Martin hearing the tapes and having nothing to lose invited them along for an audition.

A few weeks after the boys had completed their second audition Martin wrote to Epstein and offered him a recording contract. That elusive sheet of parchment was at last reality. The only bad side to the audition was the fact that George Martin didn't consider Pete Best's drumming suitable for the band. The other three were also appealing to Brian to ask Ringo Starr, the drummer to join the group. Brian was reluctant, but George Martin's hint made him realise something must be done, and so one afternoon he broke the bad news to Pete Best. He didn't want to do it, but he realised it would be best for the Beatles.

On their first actual recording session the boys put down two songs of their own: 'Love Me Do' and 'P.S. I Love You'. On October 4th, 1962 the record was unleashed upon the world, and within a matter of weeks 'Love Me Do' had reached the no. 17 position in the British charts. George Martin, who quite honestly was amazed at the progress of this record, realised the need to bring out another single quickly, and almost immediately did another session with the boys. About this time he introduced Brian to an old friend of his, Dick James.

Brian went along to meet Dick James, who at that time occupied a one-roomed office in the Charing Cross Road. Dick asked him to sit down, and takes up the story from there:

''He had with him a rough acetate of a session he had just completed with George Martin. I put it on my record player and I heard this song 'Please Please Me', and I just hit the ceiling. He asked what I thought, and I said 'I think it's a no. 1', I picked up the telephone and called a friend of mine, Philip Jones, who at that time was a light entertainment producer at ABC TV, and he was just starting a new show called *Thank Your Lucky Stars*. The breaks started to come virtually from that moment.''

The Midas Touch

Brian was suitably impressed, and agreed to let Dick have the publishing to both sides of the forthcoming disc. As it turned out Dick was right and the record did make no. 1.

The song that George Martin wanted to follow 'Love Me Do' with was in fact given to him by Dick James. A song written by an up-and-coming writer called Mitch Murray, it was entitled 'How Do You Do It?', but the Beatles couldn't get into the song so they dropped it. Brian had realised the potential of this song though, and asked the only-too-pleased Dick James if he could have it for another Liverpudlian group that he had just signed. Dick agreed, and Gerry and the Pacemakers certainly did do justice to the song and took it

right up the charts to the no. 1 spot.

And so the hits went on and on and on. Everything Brian touched turned to gold. He signed Billy J. Kramer and the Dakotas, and they too wallowed in hits. Cilla Black, the Fourmost, the Big Three, the Mersey-beats and many others followed. He formed an empire and called it NEMS (North East Music Stores), which he named after his record shop in Liverpool. Brian went on to shape the Beatles in such a way that they were shortly to have no. 1 records with everything that they released. Last but not least, they were to ultimately conquer the world.

Unfortunately, with success coming at the phenomenal rate Brian was getting it, the pressures began to grow. He started working a 25-hour day, eight days a week. He was careful not to lavish too much attention on any one act, and tried (unsuccessfully) to share his devotions. He was devoted to his artists, and saw more of them than he did of his family. One can't help feeling though, and if Brian were alive today he would probably clarify this, that the Beatles were his first love – not because they were the most successful, but because they had an affinity that Brian had never experienced before. He gave these four suburban lads the world, and gave us all the Beatles. Nobody could ask a bigger favour of anyone than that.

Sad Death

A few years later, when the Beatles were in Bangor studying meditation under the Maharishi Yogi, Brian was found dead in bed in his Mayfair house. The coroner pronounced the death as accidental, due to the cumulative effect of bromide in a drug known as Carbitol. Brian had been taking this for some time because of the ever increasing pressures, which in turn led to insomnia. The world had lost a man whose foresight was greater than any music personality before or since. The Beatles had lost more than they could have possibly imagined. Brian Epstein was a fifth Beatle. He was as much a part of them as they were of him. Words can't adequately describe the loss of a man of his stature, but perhaps the last words should come from his long time secretary Joanne Newfield:

''A lot of people seem to forget and they say 'oh he didn't do that much', but if you look at the record since his death it makes you wonder. A lot of people say that the Beatles made Brian Epstein; I don't think Brian Epstein made the Beatles, but I think he did a great deal more than he is given credit for. A lot of managers could have found a group like them and completely messed them up. It wasn't just their talent alone, it was their talent plus a very creative person behind them. Maybe business-wise he wasn't the greatest, but creatively he was a genius.''

Behind: an early picture of Epstein, the shopkeeper who conquered the pop world with the Mersey Sound.

Beatle Films

It was inevitable that the Beatles should go into films. There was already a well-beaten path from pop to movies that had been followed by Cliff Richard, Helen Shapiro and others in England, and American pop stars like Bill Haley. There was also the inevitable fact that when they did commit themselves to celluloid it would be something new, different and exciting; something that reflected the freshness of the Beatles themselves.

Almost without exception, films featuring pop stars had been shoddy, cheap, quickly made and rush-released to cash in on the artists' popularity while it lasted.

Much of the trouble lay in the fact that pop stars were demonstrably not actors. Their thespian abilities had to be taxed as little as possible, and therefore hacked-out scripts around the 'boy-meets-girl', the 'good boy rock singer misunderstood by well-meaning parents', or the 'let's do the concert right here, fellers' themes were utilized. The Beatles changed that at a stroke with *A Hard Day's Night.* They had already impressed their own unique personality on the young through their hilarious, often anarchic meetings with the press. They had a ready-made persona around which a movie could be constructed; to draw it out, to make it work cinematically they needed an empathetic director and writer.

They found him first in Richard Lester who had previously worked with Peter Sellers and Spike Milligan on the short film *The Running, Jumping And Standing Still Film.*

The marriage of Beatles and Lester was near-perfect. He saw in them elements of the Marx Brothers, cleverly disguised their lack of acting experience by allowing writer Alun Owen to exaggerate already existing traits in their personalities, and, most important, concentrated on the best natural actor of the four — Ringo.

A Hard Day's Night worked brilliantly. It was funny, had tremendous verve and pace, showed the fans the characters of the four in a glossy, lovable form and, vitally important, was packed with first-rate Beatle numbers. It was an instant success and was hailed, perhaps grudgingly, certainly with surprise, by some of the heavier critics. A follow-up was obviously indicated. *Help!* the following year was not as satisfying. The trap avoided in *A Hard Day's Night* of a plot, however slight and

bizarre, was fallen into now. The Beatles, though still central, became puppet figures amid the furious, demented action cutting from India to England, Nassau and Austria. The abilities of the many other actors swamped those of the stars, and this was to be the group's last attempt at a feature film.

The experience, however, had whetted the appetites of John and Ringo for acting and Paul for producing/directing. Lennon

worked again with Lester on *How I Won The War* and Ringo appeared in several films including *Candy, The Magic Christian* and *That'll Be The Day.* Paul, seeing any number of possibilities in the popular arts for the Beatles' talents enthused the others sufficiently to attempt their own film, this time for television — *Magical Mystery Tour.* Perhaps smarting from the critical hammering it took, the group retreated from direct involvement with movies in any

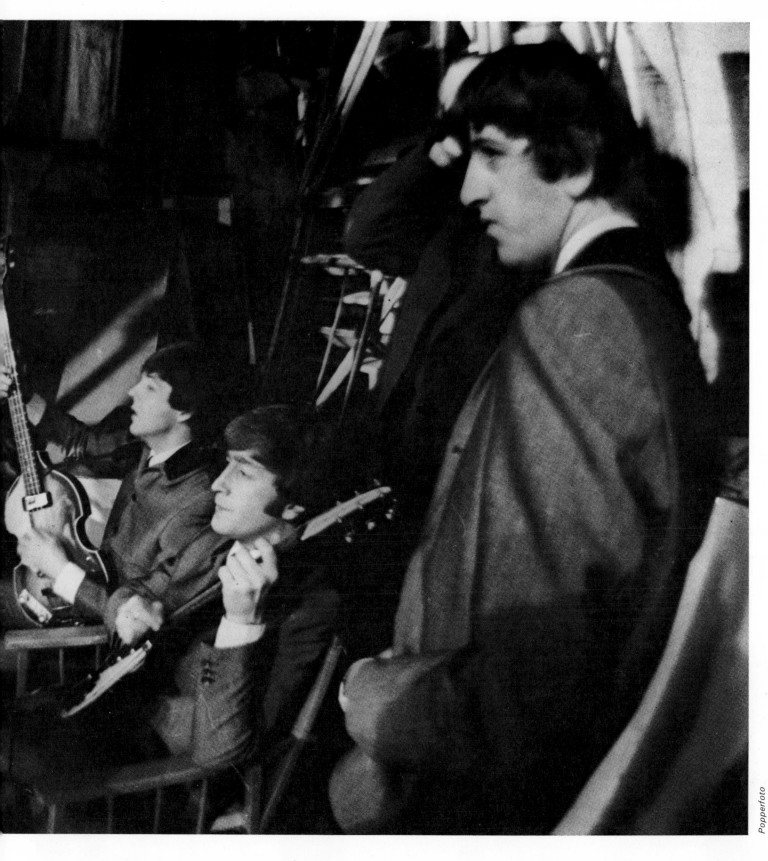

capacity other than performing; *Yellow Submarine* was a Beatle film only inasmuch as it was animation built round their characters and work; *Let It Be* was essentially a documentary showing the group at work, and it is important, when considered in the light of their break-up, which was to happen almost immediately after its release.

The Beatles' canon of movies is, regrettably, small but — typically — each film is entirely different from the others and, significantly, entirely different from any that had gone before. As in so many other things, the Beatles' films changed attitudes, especially in the movie industry. *A Hard Day's Night* and *Help!* were commercially successful and made producers think again about the so-called 'youth market'; indirectly they paved the way for *Easy Rider*, *Zabriskie Point*, *Woodstock* and many others.

The Beatles between takes on *Hard Day's Night*. Insert: 'Ticket to Ride' sequence from *Help!*

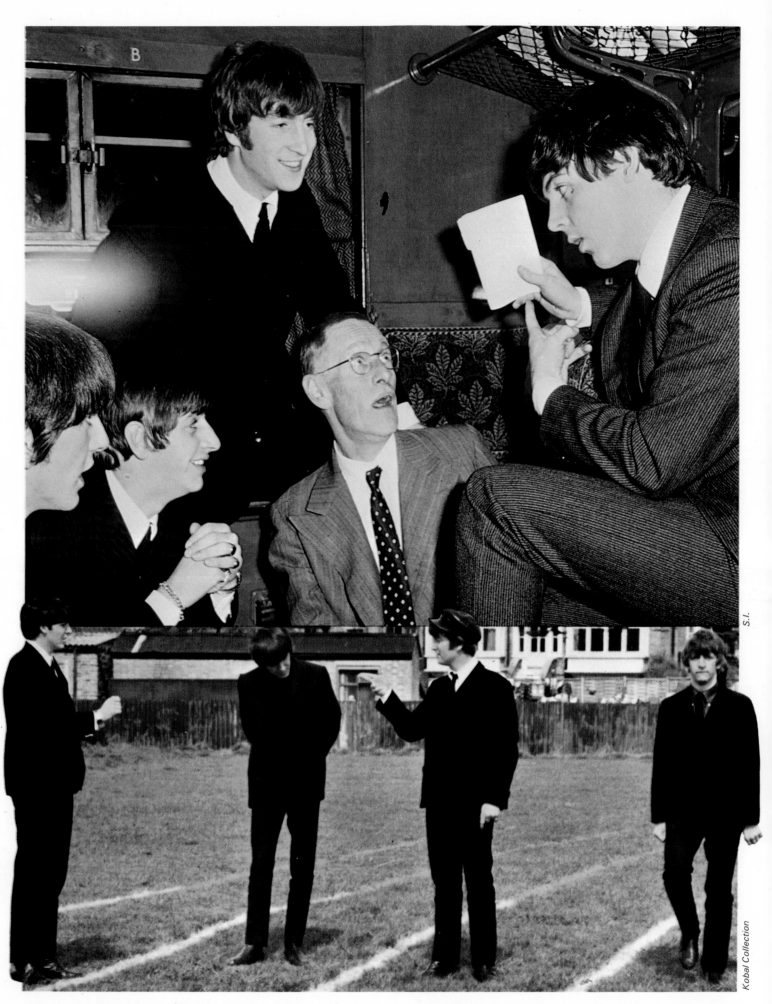

S.I.

Kobal Collection

Top: On the set with Wilfred Brambell. Below: during the filming of the 'Can't Buy Me Love' sequence.

A Hard Day's Night

Directed by Richard Lester. Starring the Beatles and Wilfred Brambell. Featuring the music of the Beatles. Original screenplay by Alun Owen.

In 1964, Brian Epstein negotiated the Beatles' first film, *A Hard Day's Night.*

To create a viable plot and capture the Liverpool vernacular, Brian Epstein had hired Liverpool's best-known playwright, Alun Owen, to write the screenplay. Alun spent a couple of days with the Beatles, picking up the way they talked, and then he dashed off the script enshrining the four stereotypes: witty John, precocious Paul, sardonic George and lovable, ordinary Ringo.

To match the energy and exuberance of the Beatles' music, Brian Epstein and producer Walter Shenson had hired Dick Lester to direct the film. Lester's style combined the slickness of a TV commercial with a surreal sense of humour which matched the Beatles' own style of buffoonery.

So, around Alun Owen's skeleton script, the film showed the Beatles taking a train to London, accompanied by Paul's grand-father, a 'very clean old man' (played by Wilfred Brambell). After evading their fans, and being shepherded around by Norm, their domineering guardian and road manager (played by Norman Rossington), they manage to escape from their hotel to visit a club. Next day they find themselves trapped again, inside a TV studio while rehearsing for their next show. The four of them break out and loon around in a field, until shooed off with the words 'I suppose you realize this is private property'. They return to the studio, but then Ringo, egged on by the 'very clean old man', again absconds for the rest of the afternoon. After wandering along the river, and striking up a friendship with a small boy, he is finally recaptured, . . . and the Beatles successfully tape their show.

The main theme of *A Hard Day's Night* was the Beatles' sense of imprisonment inside their own success. They're constantly looking for escape routes, from mobs of screaming fans, from the hotel, from the chore of autographing hundreds of photos, from the TV studio. Only occasionally, when playing their music, or during brief moments of freedom, do they begin to enjoy themselves.

Coinciding with an enthusiasm for everything British, young, and stylish, the film neatly summed up the optimistic spirit of 1964, as well as perpetuating the early Beatles' image as (in Nik Cohn's phrase) 'four ordinary, modest, no-nonsense, entirely superhuman beings'.

43

Help!

Directed by Richard Lester. Starring The Beatles, Leo McKern, Eleanor Bron. Featuring the music of the Beatles. Screenplay by Marc Behm and Charles Wood.

Glossier, more surreal than its pre-decessor, it had the advantage of colour but the disadvantage of over-slick direction. Lester moved the Beatles around locations and situations like pawns and lost their individuality as a result. The opportunity for songs hardly existed, so the breaks for music added to the unreality.

The plot centres on Ringo and a ring he wears which is coveted by a mad scientist. Although great fun and filled with excellent tunes, this second film was far less successful as a Beatle movie.

Magical Mystery Tour

Film for television by and starring the Beatles.

It was conceived and executed in haste, without any realization of the work that goes into even a short film. Its premier on British TV, Boxing Day 1967, gave the critics their first opportunity to slam the Beatles. The film was their own creation, it was unlike anything they'd ever attempted, and while it undoubtedly had good ideas and intriguing images, they had neither the experience nor the ruth-lessness needed to keep it under control.

Meanings, no doubt, can be read into it – chronologically it followed Sgt. Pepper and Epstein's death – but at first sight, it puzzled critics and audience alike and not even the songs – 'I Am The Walrus' and 'Fool On The Hill' among them – could save it. In retrospect, its reviews were perhaps rather harsher than this Beatle film deserved.

Keystone Press

Popperfoto

Popperfoto

Yellow Submarine

Animated colour cartoon featuring music by the Beatles. Directed by George Dunning.

Based loosely on the song of the same name, this was a colourful, inventive, sometimes brilliant animation of the vessel's journey, carrying the boys to Pepperland and their subsequent fight with the Blue Meanies. The group's actual involvement with the project was slight (they appeared in a brief sequence at the end) but the animators cleverly visualized the mood of the six songs included in the soundtrack. Belonging in spirit to the balmy days of 1967 and 'All You Need Is Love', it is a pleasant, if rather naive, little parable in which music and joy overcome the enemies of happiness. It showed how animation could be as modern and vital as the moment, breaking away from the whimsey of Disney.

Let It Be

Featuring the Beatles with Billy Preston. Directed by Michael Lindsay-Hogg.

The seeds of destruction were already sown and the rift was beginning to show. There was undoubtedly a need for some sort of documentary, a record of the four most phenomenal individuals at work together, doing what they knew best — making music. To that extent *Let it Be* was timely and important. It wasn't a true documentary, though; certainly it wasn't *cinéma verité,* because it was shot in a film rather than a recording studio and had one pivotal sequence filmed on the roof of the Apple headquarters.

But it was accurate in that it showed the group together, working, fooling about, unconscious of the lens. Here it was valuable because the observer could comprehend through the in-jokes, the phrases half-spoken but fully and instantly understood by each Beatle, the near-telepathy that bound together these four very different men. The camera registered the infrastructure of a brilliant team.

Other things became apparent too. There was bickering, boredom, sulkiness. There was an awareness of 'outsiders'. Paul with Linda and her daughter playing on the floor; John with the ever-present Yoko. Forces were evidently at work that would ultimately pull down the inner fabric of the group. The cameras caught this and the viewer, aware of rumour, veiled reports, press speculation and finally the split itself, could interpret the mood. The music, the film proved, was still good, strong, inventive but the spirit was crumbling. John and Paul were beginning to move far apart and the viewer's joy at the rock medleys and the new Beatle material was tinged with a sadness that such a partnership should end in acrimony.

The group's conception of the movie changed from its inception to its release — it was an Apple film but Apple was already in disarray. Paul wanted a Warhol-style freedom, Linda thought it should be a study of the Beatles. It ended up as a glossy, pretty, slightly unreal movie into which reality harshly intruded.

At one moment the group is on a roof belting out a song to the sooty air, the pigeons and office workers, at the next it is in a film studio, lovingly lit. One sequence shows four people exuberantly enjoying playing music, another shows the same people at odds with each other. It's too glossy to be real and too real to be simply an animated pin-up. In the final analysis, it is the only lengthy record we have of the Beatles at work and as such its value is immeasurable.

Towards the end — the Beatles, with Yoko Ono, listening to the songs on the soundtrack. The final tapes were later given to Phil Spector to make into an album.

A recording session on top of the 'Apple' company building in London's Savile Row. Insert: George Harrison in jocular mood.

Beatle Headlines

John Lennon Busted On Drugs Charge. That's news. The Beatles Break Up. That's news. Brian Epstein Dies. That's news. Cynthia Lennon Misses Train. That is news, too.

The Beatles were always news. No matter how trivial, far-fetched or silly the incident, it all made the headlines. If someone interpreted the 'Abbey Road' cover as proving Paul was dead, the newshounds were on to it; if John said the Beatles were more popular than Christ, the big black letters screamed it, and world reaction, across the front pages.

It's difficult for those who lived through the times to remember the impact that this group had on the news media in Britain, America and the rest of the world; it's harder still for anyone who did not experience it to believe it actually happened.

Predictably, the press were slow to catch up with the phenomenon. Long after the kids knew the Beatles were special, the papers cottoned on to the fact. The very day the media woke up can be pinpointed – October 13th, 1963. It was the day the group topped the bill on British TV's *Sunday Night At The London Palladium.* It was the first occasion that Fleet Street had experienced Beatlemania, mobbing and near riot on its own doorstep. From that moment the press interest continued unabated for five years, during which hardly a day went by without some sort of story.

No Story Too Small

No pop group – or indeed any entertainment star – in history accumulated the number of column inches in so short a time as the Beatles. They were news; hard front page news; soft downpage news; gossip column news; interview news; amusing news; cartoon material news. Almost everything they did, said, ate, drank; almost everyone they met, befriended, dated, fought or annoyed was recorded somewhere for posterity or, at least, until the following morning, the next story.

Even when the boom was well past its height in 1968, the group could not fail to hit the headlines. In one month – August – of that year alone the British press reported: that a friend of the Beatles' was buying a yacht; that cinemas round the country were dropping *Yellow Submarine*; that John was selling his Weybridge house; that George was holidaying in Corfu with thirteen friends; that Paul and girlfriend Fran Schwartz had painted the title of the group's next record on the window of the Apple shop; how Julian Lennon, aged five, was reacting to his father's romance with Yoko Ono; that Rohan O'Rahilly, the brain behind pirate Radio Caroline, was involved with Apple films; that Cynthia was suing John for divorce and naming Yoko. Trivial as most of it is, it was all considered grist to the newsman's mill. Just to get the word 'Beatles' into a headline was enough.

Although in 1968 when the tide was turning against the group (to some ill-disguised press glee), the newspapers became near-hysterical even over stories that would have been immediately 'spiked'

Below left: George marries Patti Boyd. Centre: Beatle records burnt, Georgia, 1966, in protest against John's statement that they were 'bigger than Jesus'. Opposite page left: George ordered off stage, Cleveland Ohio, 1964. Far right top: Cynthia Lennon misses the train to Bangor, 1967 on that fateful weekend of meditation with the Maharishi. Below: John peering anxiously from the train.

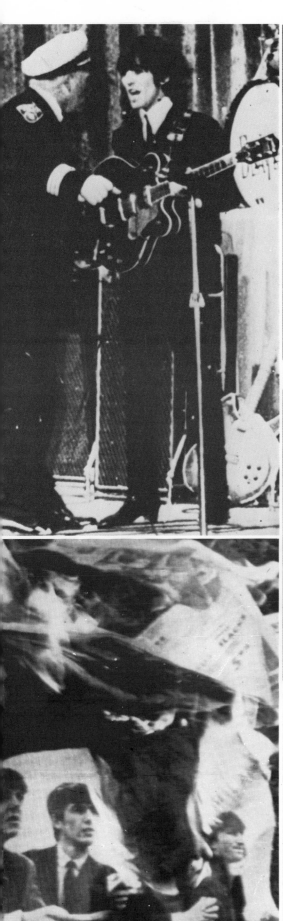

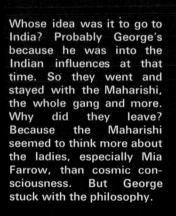

Whose idea was it to go to India? Probably George's because he was into the Indian influences at that time. So they went and stayed with the Maharishi, the whole gang and more. Why did they leave? Because the Maharishi seemed to think more about the ladies, especially Mia Farrow, than cosmic consciousness. But George stuck with the philosophy.

had they featured other groups.

The really big stories, of course, elicited actual hysteria, for example, the day that John Lennon was arrested on a drugs charge one reporter phoned Beatles' publicist Derek Taylor with two other possible headline stories for confirmation — that Freddy Lennon, John's father, was marrying, and that Yoko was pregnant. Either would have been considered worthy of a splash had the arrest not pushed other news off the front page.

Big stories like drugs busts, weddings, divorces, births, deaths, rows, the split, the court fights over the company, the sale of Northern Songs, the LSD revelations, mobbing, riots — the meat and drink of newspapers — elicited the kind of reaction in British and American press usually accorded only to royalty or the Presidency.

Something's Got To Give

The Beatles' reaction to all this changed with the years. At first, of course, they were delighted. No publicity is bad publicity when you're striving towards the top. After the first headline assault the major papers assigned special Beatle correspondents to follow them on tours abroad; the group accepted this good-naturedly, played along with the press; Ringo — held up from joining the others by illness — flew off to join them complete with a sign that, when held next to the BEA (British European Airways) livery on the plane added the letters TLES.

In time, the constant glare became wearing, tedious and disturbing; Tony Barrow, sometimes NEMS press officer, soon found his job radically altered. Instead of doing the rounds, trying desperately to get the press interested in the group, he now became a buffer, keeping newsmen away. Over-exposure can be as bad as under-exposure and a policy of selected interviews was pursued, a talk with one of the boys being accorded only to the most influential prestigious journals.

While John, George and Ringo tended to retreat from the unwelcome attentions of reporters, Paul took upon himself the role of spokesman and image builder. He understood the workings of the press better than the others, interested himself more in the ways that stories could be controlled, using the press's eagerness to their own advantage. After *Magical Mystery Tour* flopped and things started splitting at the seams even his considerable reserves of tact and diplomacy became exhausted, and the vitriol with which the press turned against the four — together and severally — forced him to withdraw from the arena.

Ten years after the crest of the wave and five after their break-up the Beatles still commanded headlines, less regularly, of course, but still more frequently than might be expected. Although press interest in others — like Bowie, the Osmonds, David Cassidy — was intense, its duration was brief. Nobody could make news like the Beatles. It was impossible to imagine, for example, the Osmonds being cracked up into national heroes on one hand — as the

Rex Features

Keystone

Top: Beatles recording live for the first-ever satellite transmission. Below: Maureen and Ringo with second son Jason. Above right: Paul marries Linda Eastman. Above far right: the 'Apple' shop in Baker Street. Below left: George and Patti Harrison arrive to answer drug charges, London 1969. Below right: John and Yoko — also on a drugs charge.

Beatles had been — and condemned on the other by a Communist paper with the line 'The Mersey Sound is the voice of 80,000 crumbling houses and 30,000 people on the dole.' No group since has stirred such emotion. No group has been able to sell newspapers.

The Beatles were at once a pressman's dream and his nightmare. His dream because any story he covered assured him of a big by-lined story; his nightmare because, as a result, a news editor would demand more of the same. No group has

commanded special colour supplements — not once but several times; has inspired editorials of praise or thunderous outrage; has prompted comparison as song writers with Schubert in an earnest weekly. But after the noise died down, what then? The thickest clippings books — if anyone had the interest or stamina to keep them up — in rock history; a mass of yellowed cuttings in some newspaper's files, telling of past glories; a record of a heady time when the press as well as the rest of the world went crazy over four men from Liverpool.

The Beatles Break Up

The Beatles' break-up marked the end of an era. The Fab Four had shaped popular music for close on a decade. Now, as four separate artists, would they be able to survive? In this, and the four following chapters, the Beatles' careers since the split tell their own story.

On April 11th, 1970, Paul McCartney announced that he had quit the Beatles.

If they had been just another pop group, there would have been no cause for alarm in Paul's statement — the others would simply have found a new bass guitarist and lead singer, and gone on roughly as before. But the Beatles' image, and their influence on pop, depended on four distinctive personalities working well together; they would not be the Beatles without Paul. From their very first album, the special quality that had lifted them above every other pop group in the world was the composing partnership of John Lennon and Paul McCartney, songwriters with a seemingly never-ending profusion of great songs that were the classics of pop.

In comparing tracks from, say, 'Please Please Me' to 'Abbey Road', it's easy to see how the Lennon/McCartney partnership had developed in seven years — they had travelled from innocence to full adult sophistication with all the trimmings of modern technology.

It was obvious that sooner or later their individual talents would draw them apart. By April 1970, George and Ringo had each made solo albums; John and Yoko had formed the Plastic Ono Band and had made several records of Lennon songs; and Paul's album with his wife Linda completed the process of separation.

But what factors actually brought about this dramatic split? It isn't difficult to imagine that virtually living in each other's pockets from 1960–69 had made their friendship and working relationship very strained. But that wasn't the main reason. One really has to see *how* they acted out their grand finale to realize the cause. And the beginning of it all started after the death of Brian Epstein.

It could be said, with all honesty, that for a time before Brian's death, his association with the Beatles was on the decline. It is thought to be because the four Beatles were experimenting with LSD and also using the Maharishi Yogi as a shoulder to lean upon. This had put them out of Brian's reach spiritually and socially, and also as they had stopped touring, he had very little to do with their public presentation. Their work was taking them into the recording studios more and the recording techniques they used were well beyond the knowledge of Brian. He started experimenting with LSD himself at about the time of 'Sgt. Pepper', and although he partook in experimental drug sessions on several occasions, it never gave him the same high as it did the other four.

Whilst the Beatles were being told about the powers of transcendental meditation by the Maharishi Yogi in Bangor, North Wales, Brian was preparing his August Bank Holiday weekend which was going to be spent in his country house in Sussex. He was preparing a gathering of friends around him to have a good time. Alas, none of his friends could make the weekend and sorrowfully, Brian returned to his London 'town house' in Belgravia. He locked himself up in his room and was never again to come out alive. On Sunday, August 27th, he was found dead in his bedroom, and a coroner pronounced his death as 'accidental', due to the cumulative effect of bromide in a drug he had taken. Within days of Brian's death, it was announced that Nems Enterprises' new chairman was to be Brian's younger brother Clive. When they heard about it, the Beatles decided that if Brian wasn't around, then nobody — brother or no brother — was going to handle them or their business affairs. The Beatles' decline and fall was just about to begin.

Torn Apart

At about the time of Brian's death, the Beatles were in the process of making a TV movie called *The Magical Mystery Tour.* By all accounts it was Paul's brainchild, and it was he who was doing all the negotiating and overall planning. It was eventually made and shown on British TV over Christmas 1967. The critics, for the first time since 1963, failed to praise a piece of work by the Beatles, and they really went to town in tearing them apart. 'Rubbish', 'Sad', 'A Dismal Performance', were just some of the headlines used to describe the Beatles' little TV fantasy. The Beatles were unhappy that the public were disappointed. Their first effort without Brian — and the press had torn them apart. It seemed to hit Paul the hardest, after all it was his idea. Was Brian's presence (or lack of it) going to prove to be a more essential ingredient to their success than most people cared to believe?

The Maharishi was slowly becoming out of favour with the group. They had taken all they needed from him, and he from them. The need for transcendental meditation was no more. They now had to find another toy to play with. So they set about formulating plans for their own company, initially, to look after their own interests. Anything else the company could do, it would do. In order to set up this new company, they were told it would cost them something in the region of £800,000. They decided to call their new toy Apple, and Apple was to manage the Beatle partnership, under terms laid down in a deed signed by the foursome in April, 1967.

So, after the formation of Apple, Paul thought that it would be a good idea to

Dezo Hoffman

and he wasn't far wrong, for although the man might have had a good working knowledge of electronics, his inventions unfortunately didn't add very much in the way of finance to Apple. Thus, outlet no. 2 was killed off.

A great deal of the Beatles' original outlay had diminished through their trust in untrained people, unable to put their talents to profitable use. It was now time for something serious to be done — and fast. The Beatles' publicist at the time, Derek Taylor, remembers the Apple heydays of 1968–69 as a continual series of frustrations — and so they must have been, for even the Beatles must have noticed the loss of around £200,000.

The film division of Apple had comparative success: they did make *Let It Be*, and this brought back more than it had laid out. When the first six-month accounts came in for the four directors to scrutinize, the Beatles decided that they had been businessmen long enough. Failure was just too hard to take.

When their first detailed accounts arrived, the accountants had to write off three company motor cars (because they were unable to verify who owned them) and thousands of pounds from advances made to various people. And this was only the period to the end of 1967, well before Apple entered its heyday.

Problems, Problems, Problems

Whilst the Beatles were locked up in their new company, Nems Enterprises, Brian's old company, was slowly sinking. Although a merchant bank and a film company were taking a financial interest in it, Clive Epstein just didn't appear to have his brother's know-how to save this sinking ship. In time Clive stood down and allowed an Australian — Robert Stigwood — to see what he could do to establish its former glory.

By January, 1969, Allen Klein and a company of New York solicitors called Eastman and Eastman had taken over the financial side of Apple to save it going into liquidation. It just so happened that the daughter of Eastman senior was none other than Linda Eastman . . . who was seeing more of Paul McCartney than either was prepared to admit at the time. It was now that the Beatles' problems really began.

Paul suggested to John that Lee Eastman become the new business manager at Apple. John was uncertain. Then Paul did something that caused a definite rift between him and the other three. For no apparent reason he purchased several thousand shares in Northern Songs — the Beatles' publishing company. Lennon was outraged, in fact he said at the time: ''It was the first time any of us had gone behind anyone else's back.'' And so it was.

The Beatles eventually met the Eastmans, and although Paul (for good reason) thought that Lee Eastman was the right man for the job, the other three begged to differ. They had their sights set on

use the company as a front for under-privileged artists. We must remember that at this time Nems (Brian's company) was still legally entitled to take 25% of the Beatles' record royalties, but as far as the four were concerned, that was where Nems was going to stop. No pin-striped suits in Apple. Oh no, this was going to be a 'hip' company. This company was going to be philanthropic for the artistically under-nourished. 'If they have a good product — we back it'.

Having sat down with men of experience and worked out where the £800,000 was going to go, it was decided that the money should be channelled through five sub-divisions. Electronics, movies, publishing, records and retailing. In a manifesto which was sent out, it was stated that the aims of Apple were to offer financial assistance

to all kinds of people with new ideas, to discover new talent, and to assist struggling artists and market inventions. Very creditable, but how long was even £800,000 going to last? People were walking into Apple's offices and coming out with cheques beyond even their belief, simply because they had managed to convince one of Apple's front-men that their invention was one day going to be considered along with those of Louis Pasteur, Alexander Fleming or Isaac Newton.

The company was taken for a ride on many fronts. The retailing side of the company, through a London shop, lost a great deal of money; and the company's electronic division was also going through similar grief. John Lennon once described one protégé as 'the original mad inventor', another New York businessman – Allen Klein.

Klein was an accountant who had the reputation of being very forthright and hard. If he thought something, he said it. He didn't care who he upset. Everyone in the pop world knew Klein was a hard bargainer. Klein had, in fact, gone to enormous lengths to get in touch with Lennon to ask him if he could help them sort out their financial problems, and after several days he managed to arrange a meeting with John and Yoko Ono at the Dorchester Hotel in London.

Lennon remembers that first meeting: "I remember that he knew all about the Beatles and their music, and that impressed me. It was more than the East-mans knew. As soon as we had spoken for about half an hour I knew he was the man to get us out of our rut."

A meeting the following day at the Apple HQ saw an interesting occurrence take place. Lennon stormed into the room and told the others that Klein was the man for him. Paul was a little taken aback with this intrusion. The other two asked John why he felt so strongly, and he told them of his meeting with Klein 24 hours previously. He told them that Klein was going to look into his financial affairs immediately, and Ringo and George said that they too would like Klein to perform this service for them. Paul walked out of the meeting.

After that fateful gathering, it became known that a war within Apple had broken out. It was Paul McCartney and the East-mans versus Lennon, Harrison, Starr and Klein; furthermore it didn't look as though the situation was going to end in a friendly way. It was even rumoured that this could not only be the end of the Beatles, but that the entire episode could end up in a court.

Freed From Nems

While the Beatles' 'internal' battle was going on, Klein was busy in London trying to free the Beatles from Nems who, although doing nothing for the Beatles, were still legally entitled to a share of all Beatle record royalties. The Beatles, or namely John, George and Ringo, didn't like the Nems arrangement, and asked Klein if he could sort it out. Sure enough, after many months of bargaining he freed the Beatles from Nems and at the same time made substantial capital investments for them.

From this point onwards, problem piled on top of problem and the battle got bigger and bigger. The Beatles were still making records both together and solo, but the general public began to realize that the end was nigh. Tension between the group, needless to say, was getting greater, and there was no better example of that than in the studio sequence of their film *Let It Be*, where harsh words travelled between McCartney and Harrison.

John Lennon married Yoko Ono and Paul married Linda Eastman within days of each other, and it appears that both the ladies had their own ideas of how the

61

music of their respective husbands should take shape. To an extent they both succeeded.

'Abbey Road' was the last album that the Beatles recorded together, and it sold like hot cakes. Although 'Let It Be' came out after 'Abbey Road', it was nevertheless recorded long before. The tension certainly didn't come through on 'Abbey Road', and many Beatle addicts in fact consider it their best album. It was noted at about this time that besides having vastly different opinions about who should be taking charge of their money, etc, John and Paul were – in company with their respective wives – also moving in opposite musical directions.

The *coup de grace* – as far as the Beatles were concerned – was the feuding that took place when Paul wanted his solo album, 'McCartney', issued about the same time as the 'Let It Be' album. Therefore possibly jeopardizing sales of the latter. This caused enormous arguments between McCartney and the other three plus Klein.

At Loggerheads

Their relationships with each other were at the lowest ebb ever, with no end in sight. McCartney thought that the release of his solo album had very little to do with Klein; but Klein thought otherwise. As if this wasn't causing enough furore, McCartney also objected strongly to the instructions Klein had given to Phil Spector with regard to one of his songs on the 'Let It Be' album. Strings and schmaltz were not what Paul had intended when he wrote 'Long And Winding Road', and besides that, no manager was entitled to interfere directly with their music in Paul's eyes.

Yes, it could be said that the Beatle Era had now ended. It had, unfortunately, ended on a very sad note – in a courtroom in London. Justice Stamp, in delivering a long opinion prior to appointing a receiver to take charge of the Beatles & Co. partnership, made only passing references to their music. He paid little attention to the Beatles' musical disputes, as this was out of his sphere, but he did go into great detail about management quarrels and other differences of opinion. A great deal of attention was paid to Allen Klein. To quote Justice Stamp: ''It seems that the controversy in this action centres around both the personality and activities of Mr. Klein.''

Paul McCartney had backed his case for the appointment of a receiver with four main arguments. He declared that the Beatles had long since ceased to perform as a group; that his artistic freedom was liable to be interfered with so long as the partnership existed; that no partnership accounts had been prepared since the Beatles had entered into their deed of partnership in April, 1967; and that the other three Beatles had sought to impose upon him a manager whom he found unacceptable.

Justice Stamp found Paul's case a valid one, and appointed a receiver to take

A resolute looking Paul McCartney, with Linda during the Beatles case, in 1971.

Keystone

charge of the Beatles' affairs. In May 1971, John, George and Ringo accepted Paul's decision to leave the group and all decided not to appeal against the court's decision to let him do so. Mr Morris Finer Q.C., representing Apple, said later that his clients (Starr, Harrison and Lennon) considered that in the circumstances it was in their best interests to consider means whereby McCartney could disengage himself from the partnership. Subsequently, Paul left the Beatles.

Much bad feeling went on between the four Beatles after the matter was taken to court. John and Yoko settled in America, Paul and Linda in Scotland. The latter two formed a band, Wings, and took them on the road with enormous success. As time passed, Klein was hoisted from his managerial position by, ironically, John, George and Ringo. The whole time these events were happening, George and Ringo were merrily making records and keeping out of the headlines. If it was difficult for any ex-Beatle to stay out of the press, they managed to do so for months on end, only appearing in print when they had a new offering for sale.

On a happier note, in December, 1973, Paul and John were communicating frequently between Britain and the States, and at last the squabbles that broke the band up seemed to be history. Both

admired each other's records, and both expressed a desire to play together again. In January 1974, the Home Office granted Paul a visa to the States. (He was unable to go previously due to a drug offence.) For the first time since the big split, John and Paul met and discussed the possibilities of a reunion, along with George and Ringo, in order to make some music. Upon hearing the news, the music world went crazy. Could it be true? Would they still have mass appeal? Could they pick up where they left off? These were some of the questions that were being asked. Of course, everyone would love to see these four musical magicians back on stage or on the same record, playing together again. If they could get back at least some of their old harmony, they could possibly make some of their greatest music ever, each one enriched with so many varied experiences and with so much more to give.

George Martin was once heard to say: ''I don't think Linda is any substitute for John, in the same way as I don't think that Yoko is any substitute for Paul.''

The Beatles' break-up was one of the saddest moments in the history of pop. It could be comparable to the death of Buddy Holly. The only difference being, you can't bring Buddy Holly back to life. The Beatles? Well that's another matter.

John Lennon: A Man Who Cares

When the Beatles sang for the Queen and Prince Philip at the annual Royal Variety Show in London in 1963, it was John Lennon who invited the audience to join in with the words . . . ''Those of you in the cheaper seats — clap your hands, and those of you in the more expensive seats — just rattle your jewellery.'' Like a court jester, Lennon was taking the opportunity to lay down some hard social truths from behind a joker's mask.

Right from the Beatles' first public appearances John Lennon had been type-cast as the aggressive intellectual of the group. Stories abounded of his art college days in Liverpool, when he would roam around town 'like a wounded buffalo', getting drunk and having heavy arguments. Later, Brian Epstein might have made the Beatles wash their hair more often, wear suits, and stop swearing in front of their audience, but he could never completely stop Lennon from shooting his mouth off.

In 1966 however, John found himself in deep water when he told a London newspaper that the Beatles were more popular than Jesus. In Britain, no one

L.F.I.

Top left-hand picture: Lennon, with the Plastic Ono Band on British TV in 1969. Below: John and Yoko in various stages of undress, as they try to show the press how sincere they are.

C. Walters

seemed to even blink at the remark, but in the southern states of the US such words were taken as blasphemy. In Alabama, Beatles' records and effigies were burnt in public and their songs were banned by several radio stations – all this on the eve of their final American tour. Brian Epstein hurriedly issued a statement watering down Lennon's remark, apologies were made, and the Beatles survived the tour without being burnt as heretics. In fact, the tour was their most profitable of all, but by then they had had enough. They decided to give up performing as a live band in order to concentrate on their recordings, and pursue their separate interests. This decision was quickly justified by the brilliant 'Sgt. Pepper' album in 1967, and the lavish critical praise it collected. Then, in August of that year, while the Beatles were meditating with the Maharishi in India, the world was shocked to hear of the death of Brian Epstein.

Separate Superstars

In quick succession the Beatles had both given up the gruelling tours which had cemented them together, and lost the man who had protected their clean, innocent image from the sarcasm of the press. Four very different minds, previously concealed under 'Mop-Top' haircuts, went their separate ways. As a result, 'The Beatles' double-album, 'Let It Be' and 'Abbey Road' contain simply Lennon songs, McCartney songs, and Harrison songs, played with great skill, but without the alchemy that had previously blended their four minds into one. The Beatles disintegrated into four separate superstars who continued to pool their backing roles – drums, bass, rhythm and lead guitars – but stopped sharing their identity.

While Paul McCartney took on Brian Epstein's job of being tactful to the press and thinking up new Beatles' enterprises, and George Harrison retreated from the limelight to concentrate on his music and religion, John Lennon's identity quickly developed along the lines of the angry artist.

John had always been the Beatle with whom intellectuals loved to flirt and had published two slim volumes of drawings and verse that had drawn critical comparison with James Joyce and Lewis Carroll. Now, though, he was going far beyond the role of the pop poet. His marriage to Cynthia broke down in 1968 and John met Yoko Ono – a veteran of the New York experimental art world who created events and art happenings designed to disturb people or make them question the way in which they saw the world. John and Yoko were married in Gibraltar in March 1969, and then flew to Vienna where they invented a new form of

BAGISM

Keystone

64

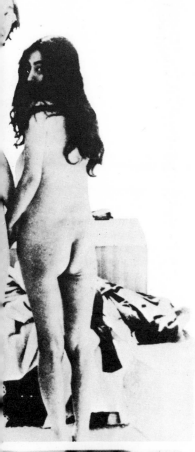

communication by holding a press conference from inside a gigantic bag, which John later commented on:

"The reporters all stood back saying 'Is it really John and Yoko?' and 'What are you wearing and why are you doing this?' We said, 'This is total communication with no prejudice'."

John then started supporting every unpopular cause he came across, outraging public opinion and doing the unexpected. To announce his love for Yoko, they made a record together of sound experiments, put it inside a sleeve showing John and Yoko holding hands, stark naked, and called it 'Two Virgins', released in November 1968. Instead of communicating the love they had found together, John and Yoko made themselves vulnerable to every accusation from childishness to obscenity, and Lennon looked like becoming the first pop star to be destroyed by public ridicule . . .

'The way things are going
They're gonna crucify me'

. . . he sang hopefully on 'The Ballad Of John And Yoko' in May 1969, the last single that John and Paul recorded together. Then, in November 1969, John took another step towards martyrdom when he returned his MBE award to the Queen, accompanied by a note explaining that he was protesting against British involvement in the wars in Biafra and Vietnam, and protesting against 'Cold Turkey' slipping down the charts.

Bed-In For Peace

'Cold Turkey' was a single that John and Yoko had recorded with the Plastic Ono Band in October '69 — a group of musical friends whose membership changed with every recording that they made. John started the group at a time when differences of opinion between the Beatles were increasing as he kept coming up with songs that the other Beatles showed little enthusiasm for. The Plastic Ono Band's first single was 'Give Peace A Chance', a repetitive rock mantra recorded in the Queen Elizabeth Hotel in Montreal. John and Yoko had arrived in Montreal after flying round the world campaigning for peace by lying in bed for a week in various hotels. They called the campaign a 'Bed-In,' and when they reached Montreal, John and Yoko and various friends in the hotel room, including Timothy Leary and the Radha Krishna Temple, recorded this new anthem for the peace movement.

The second Plastic Ono single, 'Cold Turkey', was a much more frightening record, featuring Eric Clapton's howling lead guitar and lyrics that screamed of the pain of heroin withdrawal. Of course, John Lennon's pain went a lot deeper than taking a few drugs. The public were becoming more and more confused and alienated by John and Yoko's antics. Everything they did seemed to land them in the headlines or in the courtroom, and

C. Walter

Ono Band singles, used an hypnotic, constantly changing rock & roll rhythm to sing about the light that lay at the end of the tunnel:

*'Instant Karma's gonna get you
Gonna look you right in the face
You better get yourself together darlin'
Join the human race'*

'Instant Karma' was the first single that Phil Spector produced for Lennon, and out of the simplest ingredients they created a classic for the '70s. The lyrics summoned up instant enlightenment in the same way that the 20th Century has already given us instant coffee and instant pain-killers and Alan White's brilliant drumming drove the message home with a strangely fractured dance rhythm. But most of all it was Lennon's voice, multiplied into an entire choir by Spector's subtle use of echo, that transformed the song into something both magical and desperate.

Raw Emotion

Magic and desperation. Those two qualities have always been present in Lennon's work, and his greatest songs happened when the two became fused into one, as in 'Strawberry Fields Forever' or 'I Am The Walrus'. Lennon always used more raw emotion in his songs than Paul McCartney, who tended to create short stories or cameo portraits in song form. Many of John's Beatle songs, such as 'I'm A Loser' and 'Help!', had worked on two different levels. To the public they appeared to be good, bouncy songs in the boy-loses-girl tradition. You could tap your feet to the rhythm and the tune stayed in your head forever. But inside these songs, John was also screaming that his Beatle image was suffocating him. The Beatles seemed to be four cuddly boys-on-the-block, lively but harmless, and Lennon felt stifled:

*'Although I laugh and I act like a clown
Beneath this mask I am wearing a frown*

('I'm A Loser')

The antics of John and Yoko were confusing, and sometimes pathetic, but it was a stage Lennon had to go through to tear up his old image in full public view, so that he could start again as John Lennon rather than John the Beatle.

The final move in this re-birth came when John and Yoko received therapy from the radical American psychologist Dr. Arthur Janov. Usually, psychoanalysis or therapy is a long and difficult process, but Janov believed people could free themselves from their fears and hang-ups in one decisive breakthrough. He forced his patients to re-live their most painful and difficult experiences, and, hopefully, the patient would respond with a scream of liberation: a 'primal scream'.

John Lennon came from a broken home. He had been brought up by his Aunt Mimi, who disapproved of his

BACK TRACK

1968, June: John's marriage to Cynthia breaks down. John and Yoko become good friends. **October:** John arrested for possession of cannabis in his Marylebone flat. **November:** John and Yoko release 'Two Virgins' album with cover photo of themselves naked.
1969, March: John marries Yoko in Gibraltar. They fly to Amsterdam for first 'Bed-In' for peace. **July:** John releases his first non-Beatle single 'Give Peace A Chance', recorded in Montreal. **October:** 'Cold Turkey' single released by Plastic Ono Band with Eric Clapton. **November:** John returns his MBE to protest against British involvement in Vietnam and Biafra wars. **December:** 'Live Peace In Toronto' album of Plastic Ono Band (with Clapton) performing at Toronto Rock & Roll Festival.
1970, February: John releases 'Instant Karma' single produced by Phil Spector. **March:** Exhibition of John's lithographs seized by police on grounds of indecency. **Summer:** John and Yoko receive 'primal scream' therapy from Dr. Janov in Los Angeles. **December:** Paul files suit demanding dissolution of the Beatles. John releases 'John Lennon/Plastic Ono Band' announcing 'The dream is over'.
1971, March: 'Power To The People' single from John & POB. **September:** John releases 'Imagine' album. **December:** 'Happy Xmas (War Is Over)' single from John & POB & Harlem Community Choir.
1972, September: 'Some Time In New York City' (plus Live Jam) album by John and Yoko and Plastic Ono Band and Elephant's Memory.
1973, March: US Immigration Department order Lennon's deportation. 'Pardon Lennon' movement launched. **November:** 'Mind Games' album.
1974, September: 'Whatever Gets You Through The Night' single. 'Walls And Bridges' LP.

when a London art gallery exhibited John's drawings, they were — predictably — visited by the police and charged with displaying obscene art. At the same time, Lennon had a short haircut and auctioned off his long tresses to raise money for the Black Panthers. John and Yoko, meanwhile, were periodically climbing back into their bags and announcing that Hanratty, the last man to be executed in Britain, was really innocent and should be posthumously pardoned.

None of this endeared them to the

public. Vicious remarks were made against Yoko Ono, partly because she was a woman with a mind of her own, partly because she was Japanese; but also because people were puzzled and frightened by the games that she and John were playing in public. If you believed what the papers were saying, it was as though Lennon was determined to destroy what was left of his mass popularity. And yet, among all this pain and confusion, he was still making great music.

'Instant Karma', the best of the Plastic

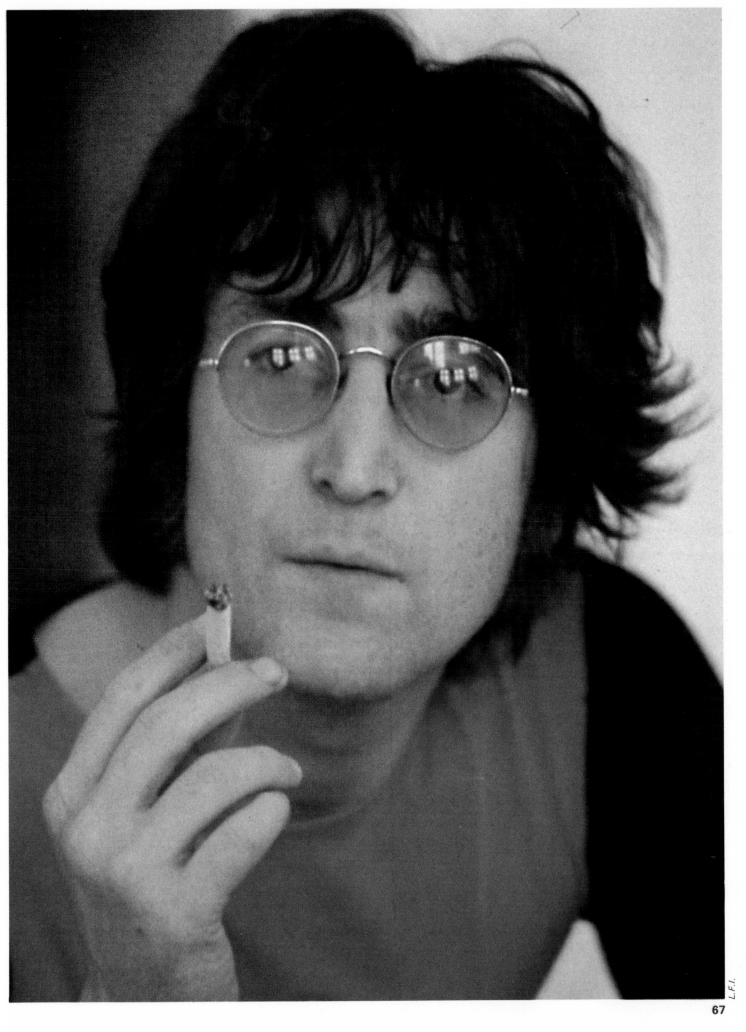

L.F.I.

Teddy-Boy looks and obsession with pop music, and when he was 18, his mother had been killed in a car crash. All this had left a deep scar on his mind, and then he had been catapulted into world-wide fame. For five Beatlemaniac years he had been struggling to keep his own personality together, while the world tried to turn him into a cuddly Mop Top.

Plastic Pop Idol

So John went through Janov's treatment, and out of his experiences he created the 'John Lennon/Plastic Ono Band' album, on which he sang about losing his mother, about being a plastic pop idol, and about a world that was ruled by greed and prejudice. The album was everything the Beatles weren't — it was hysterical, it was violent, it was politically committed — and it worked brilliantly. In the hands of a lesser artist these ideas might have been embarrassing or simply bizarre. Lennon made them work by using three separate areas of his life. He used the rawest form of rock music and screaming vocals — the same scream he had used on 'Twist And Shout' and 'Help!' — but now he screamed something real and personal, instead of an imaginary boy-loses-girl misery. He used his experience as a Beatle to explain, in 'Working-Class Hero', that although the world had made him an idol and a millionaire, he felt neither free nor happy, because he had been used. The Beatles, he was saying, had been played up as heroes and success stories to distract people from their own problems:

'Keep you doped with religion and sex
    and TV
And you think you're so clever and
    classless and free
But you're still . . . peasants as far as
    I can see'

He used the loss of his mother to describe a pain that every one of his audience had felt: the pain of separating from home and family, the pain of experiencing the world as a lonely and competitive place. And Lennon balanced all this pain against the love he had found with Yoko: the belief that people *could* reach each other and help each other, when free from illusions. Lennon was saying that the Beatles had been a beautiful dream, and it was now time to wake up.

It was a powerful statement, and for some it was too raw and aggressive to swallow easily. So Lennon's next album, 'Imagine' in October '71, repeated these beliefs, but phrased them in music that had more traditional beauty: lush strings and haunting melodies. The title song suggested discarding all the illusions which got in the way of world unity:

'Imagine there's no countries
It isn't hard to do
Nothing to kill or die for
And no religion too'

Top: John, with his girlfriend, May Pang, at James Cagney's Life Achievement award ceremony in Hollywood. Opposite: John with his friend Harry Nilsson being shown the door after a disturbance at Ciro's nightclub on Sunset Strip.

. . . but the words were set in a sensuously beautiful tune and cushioned by banks of violins, so it was hard to resist the spell of the music. 'Imagine' also contained the sinister 'How Do You Sleep?' — the most controversial song written by an ex-Beatle. To the average listener it amounted to a violent and sneering attack on Paul McCartney, who was criticized for making vacuous muzak, obeying all his wife's whims (something which Lennon had often been criticized for), and being a washed-out talent. The song even began with audience noises and violins tuning up — just like the beginning of 'Sgt. Pepper', the album on which the Beatles had pooled their personalities and musical talents most successfully.

The song seemed impossible to justify. It was John Lennon's carefully calculated attempt to hurt his former best friend as deeply as possible, and it made nonsense of Lennon's preaching about love and harmony. Yet for two reasons, it worked. Musically it was brilliant, regardless of what it was saying. The eerie violin riffs, one of George Harrison's most menacing guitar solos, Nicky Hopkins' funky piano, and Lennon's sneering vocal, were combined by Spector's adroit production into an elegant musical nightmare. More importantly, the song was Lennon's way of pointing out he was still human, and could still be overwhelmed by irrational and spiteful emotions. John Lennon still contained a mass of contradictions, and he tried to understand them by exposing them — rather than coming on like a glib salesman for peace and love.

After 'Imagine', John and Yoko settled

down in Greenwich Village as permanent members of the New York scene, and in many ways John created an American version of his life as a Beatle. Allen Klein was his financial adviser, doing Brian Epstein's old job. Phil Spector was his producer and musical godfather, the part once played by George Martin. And his constant companion and collaborator was Yoko, instead of Paul. Lennon wanted to experience a different scene, and he and Yoko were also trying to find Kyoko, Yoko's daughter from her first marriage who had been brought up by Yoko's divorced husband. They dedicated several songs to the lost child, and the search caused them a lot of pain and frustration.

Out of their new life, John and Yoko created 'Some Time In New York City' released in September '72, a musical diary about the people they met and the issues they were involved with. The album cover resembled the front page of the *New York Times,* and John and Yoko attempted to write an anthem for every radical cause that caught their eye. Women's Lib, Angela Davies, the Attica Prison shooting, the British troops in Northern Ireland — everyone got a song, and yet the total effect was curiously empty. 'John Lennon/ Plastic Ono Band' and 'Imagine' had worked because the politics and the ideas had flowed from John's personal experiences, never sounding like a newspaper headline or a glib slogan. But on 'Some

Time In New York City', John and Yoko seemed to be echoing every liberal slogan they had heard in New York's radical-chic penthouses. It was hard to believe they knew or cared much about their subjects, especially since their lyrics were so facile and they managed to somehow preach passionate support for at least 10 different causes at once.

Lennon seemed to realise this, for 'Mind Games', his next album released in November '73, concentrated again on his own thoughts and emotions. Compared with his first post-Beatle recording, 'Mind Games' was a very mellow piece of work. Instead of screams or musical hysteria, Lennon used a more delicate approach to instrumentation, and the lyrics dissolved political struggles and the fight to preserve one's balance into images of continual cosmic evolution:

*'So keep on playing those mind games
  forever
Doing the ritual dance in the sun
Millions of mind guerillas
Putting their soul power to the karmic
  wheel'*

Pushing Forward Boundaries

A handful of innovators have made the story of pop music something more important than a list of hit parades and a museum of teenage fashions. By pushing forward the boundaries of what could be

expressed in song, how it could be said in music, and the relationship between songs and society, they have made pop chronicle the anger, the ambitions, and the fantasies of millions of young people.

On these counts it is arguable that John Lennon was the most important innovator of the late '60s and early '70s. He explored whole areas of psychology, politics, and personal fantasy, without losing contact with the roots of pop or with his audience. And he backed up everything he sang with the way he lived. His voice remained as earthy and exciting as when he sang 'Twist And Shout', and he has created hundreds of good tunes, from 'Please Please Me' to 'Mind Games'.

Since the break-up of the Beatles, Paul, George and Ringo have all continued making fine records — but within a narrow range of music and emotions. They've given their followers a lot of pleasure, but few surprises. John has been the most ambitious, the most unstable, and the most interesting. A clear thread of anger, idealism, and rock & roll has run right through his antics and his different albums. As he summed it all up on the single 'Instant Karma':

*'Why in the world are we here?
Surely not to live in pain and fear
Why on earth are you there?
When you're everywhere
Come and get your share!'*

Paul McCartney:
The Wing Commander

Reference to the *Oxford Concise Dictionary* gives the meaning of 'super' as: 'exceeding, going beyond, more than, too exalted for contact and beyond the norm'. Turning the pages reveals the meaning of the word 'star' as: 'principal item in a performance or an entertainment, brilliant or prominent person, such a body that appears in groups of two, four or six'.

Having determined the literal meaning of 'superstar', it's easy to appreciate how all of these meanings can apply to Paul McCartney; and easy to understand exactly why he is often classed as such.

Trumpeting Start

For someone who showed little interest in music as a child, Paul must have surprised everyone when he persuaded an uncle to loan him a trumpet so he could pick out little tunes on it. Then, after acquiring a taste for the trumpet, Paul started doodling about with the family piano situated in the living-room. But it was only with the arrival of rock & roll that Paul's interest in music proper was aroused. Having witnessed a concert by Lonnie Donegan at the Liverpool Empire, Paul persuaded his father to buy him a guitar. His father, himself a keen musician, purchased a second-hand six-string for £15, and Paul's assault on pop music — a lot of which he was to change — had begun.

He began listening to records and the radio as much as possible. His favourite listening was Elvis, Little Richard and all the other American rock & rollers. Having listened to 'All Shook Up' over and over again, he began to pick out the chords on his guitar — which by this time he had converted into a left-handed model — and having learnt the chords, he started trying vocal imitations of Elvis' voice.

The next song he learnt came easier than the first, and the one after that, easier
Joseph Stevens

still. Paul began to realize that playing the guitar wasn't as difficult as it first looked; so, with a miniature repertoire of his own, he went out in search of other musicians who shared his devotion to rock & roll.

He didn't have to look very far. One afternoon a close friend dragged Paul along to the local parish church to listen to a group that he sometimes played with. Paul listened to the group and criticized them harshly — which for someone who'd never played out in front of an audience was a bit of a cheek. He did, however, remember that the lead guitarist was quite good (meaning by his own standards) . . . and that was the first meeting of Paul McCartney and John Lennon.

Paul Joins John

Having exchanged mutual likes and dislikes, Paul told John that he too could play a guitar. John showed typical Lennonesque interest, and invited Paul along to the group's next rehearsal which was to be later that week. At the rehearsal Paul, armed with guitar, showed John all the chords he knew; and John in return did the same for Paul. Paul couldn't help noticing that John played all his chords in banjo structures, and later learnt that this was because John had learned the guitar via the banjo. Nonetheless, Paul was invited to take part in the rehearsal — he was the most fluent player of them all — and immediately afterwards John asked Paul to join the group.

After John and Paul had been playing together for some months, they decided to expand their repertoire. The only songs they knew, though, were either the ones they had heard on the radio, or ones which either of them had on record. John explained to Paul that he had written a few little songs that maybe they could include in their act. Paul listened attentively, and liked what he heard. It had never occurred to Paul McCartney that songs had to be written in order to be performed, and for the first time in his 16-year-old life he considered the possibilities of writing some of his own. Little did he know that in his field he possessed the talent of the supernatural.

The first few songs he wrote were not very good. He found that he was able to write so much, but that when, for example, he got to the middle, he was lost. At this point he turned to his friend and, in his eyes, 'experienced' songwriter, John Lennon. John willingly helped Paul over the hump by writing in chords that had never before occurred to Paul. The result(?) . . . the first Lennon/McCartney compositions.

By this time the group had undergone major changes. The other original members had left, and a new guitarist — George Harrison — had joined. They also had Stu Sutcliffe on bass and, later, Pete Best on drums. They were playing raucous rock & roll with all the venom and drive of enthusiastic youngsters having a good laugh. But this group meant more than a good laugh to these 'kids'; they were serious,

they believed that they could make it big. All they needed, so they thought, was a good image, the right music and a lot of luck . . . and they could be as big as Elvis. But we all have our dreams!

The band, with Paul and John very much the leaders, moved on from clubs in and around Liverpool to Hamburg. The apprenticeship was taking place. Working long hours and, when not on stage, sitting in their room writing, they polished up their stage act. Furthermore, they were by now building up a fan following. Nobody, but nobody, and this included even Paul's parents, was going to tell them that they couldn't make it.

When, as the Beatles, they did begin to break the ice, it was Paul who acted as the group's go-between to the general public that wanted to get to them. Paul was, unofficially, the Beatles' public relations man: he did most of the talking during interviews, answering the serious questions seriously, and always managing to appear in spontaneous photographs as though he had spent at least three hours preparing for them.

Everyone had their particular favourite Beatle, but most people seemed to harbour a kind of affection for Paul. Perhaps it was because of his boy-next-door look, or perhaps that he never seemed too exalted for contact, but most probably it was because of the songs he wrote.

Parent Appeal

Paul seemed to have the uncanny knack of being able to write songs aimed directly at the hearts of his audience . . . a talent he doesn't appear to have lost. John, on the other hand, was even then writing far more about his inner self, and the fans found it just a little bit too difficult to associate his stuff with themselves. But this is generalizing of course. Paul's songs also had, it appears, far more meaning for the Mums and Dads, and it was, after all, once the Mums and Dads started taking an interest in the Beatles that the affair blew up out of all proportion.

How easily a married couple of 50, for example, could identify with 'When I'm 64', 'She's Leaving Home', 'Honey Pie' and 'Here, There And Everywhere'. Because Paul sang them with great care and flavour these people made Paul, in their minds at least, a superstar. Like Frank Sinatra before him — and Tom Jones after — Paul had the charisma that makes people of all ages, colours, and sexes, warm to him. He appears to say in his music what everyone would like to say to each other, but can never find the words to express.

Then, when Brian Epstein died in 1967, the Beatles unconsciously became Paul McCartney's group. It was Paul who took over the running and musical direction of the group, and in many ways this signalled the beginning of the end for the Beatles. All four of them were by then writing in different directions, and it was plainly obvious that it wouldn't be long before the party was over.

But in order to keep the party going,

BACK TRACK

Born on June 18th, 1940 at Walton Hospital, Liverpool.
1969, Paul and Linda Eastman marry at Marylebone Registry Office, London.
1970, April: Paul's first solo album 'McCartney' released. December: the Beatles split up and Paul issues a court suit in order to get the Beatles dissolved.
1971, February: Paul & Linda release

their first single entitled 'Another Day', making the UK Top 10. May: Paul and Linda release first album together entitled 'Ram'. From this album 'Back Seat Of My Car' on single, flopped. December: Wings' first album released entitled 'Wild Life'.
1972, February: Wings release 'Give Ireland Back To The Irish' which is immediately banned by the BBC. Start of 'Wings Over Europe' tour. May: 'Mary Had A Little Lamb' single which

climbs into the UK Top 10. December: Wings release 'Hi, Hi, Hi' which again is banned by the BBC, this time for sexual references.
1973, May: Paul plays to a British audience for the first time since 1966 at Bristol Hippodrome, beginning a UK tour, followed by a UK TV spectacular. Wings' second album 'Red Rose Speedway' and from it a single 'My Love' is released. June: Paul writes music for James Bond film *Live And Let Die*. The

song is also released as a single. October: 'Helen Wheels' released as single. November: Wings' third album 'Band On The Run' released and highly acclaimed by the press. Denny Seiwell and Henry McCullough leave Wings, to rejoin later in the next year. December: McCartney family compère the Christmas Walt Disney TV show.
1974, Paul's US Visa granted by Home Office – rumours of Beatles reunion. November: 'Junior's Farm' single.

Main picture: Wings, featuring Paul McCartney in the foreground and in the background, Linda McCartney and Denny Laine. Insert, L.H. pic: Linda, Paul and Denny in a London recording studio late in 1973. R.H. pic: The McCartney family (Mary and baby Stella) are definitely 'on the bus'. Here, they cuddle up together as they wing their way round Europe for their 1973 tour: only big sister Heather is missing.

The McCartneys relax on their private bus while on the 'Wings Over Europe' tour of 1973.

Paul decided to make a film based on a magical mystery tour that he would plan, organize and see through. While the others were all doing their own things, Paul was busy working on — what was for him — his first major venture not directly linked with the other three. Unfortunately, press-wise, the project failed; or if it didn't fail, it failed to reach the required standards. But then, it was the Beatles who had set these standards.

Even though the TV film didn't do as well as everyone would have liked, Paul nevertheless came up with two classic songs: 'Your Mother Should Know' and 'Fool On The Hill'. These, like others before them, hit right upon the heart-strings of people all over the world.

Beatles Split Up

George, meanwhile, had gone into meditation and mysticism, John had met up with a Japanese avant-garde artist who was leading him into sacks, brown paper bags and a wild life-style, Ringo had left the limelight, and — to the people who make or break superstars — Paul was the only one who seemed to have retained any sanity.

Eventually, as all had expected, the Beatles split up. It was Paul who filed a court suit demanding the dissolution of the group, and just after he filed it he said: "For me I want to get out of the contract, I think the group is finished. We have split, and everything we have ever earned or that we were ever in should be divided equally. But the others don't agree. They think it should continue exactly as it was. If the three of them wanted to they could sit down today and write on a little piece of paper and I would be released. That is all I want."

The suit passed through court and Paul McCartney became detached from Ringo, John and George . . . free to do as he wished. Whether he would disappear into retirement or form himself another group, nobody was sure. But one thing that had sadly ended for good was the writing partnership of John Lennon and Paul, a partnership that had written so many classic hit tunes.

Much of the initial 'split-up' problem came from the fact that Paul, so typically, had made a solo album which he wanted to release at the same time as 'Let It Be'. The administrative king at Apple, Allan Klein, was worried that this solo effort

from McCartney would offset the sales of 'Let It Be', a venture in which Mr Klein had a possible large financial return. 'McCartney' was, nevertheless, released, and it sold well without noticeably offsetting the sales of the group effort.

For people who had been saying that McCartney without Lennon just wasn't going to work, the release of this solo effort must have come as a great surprise. 'Maybe I'm Amazed' was a classic McCartney song, and in silent ways made it clear that Paul was quite content not only to work on his own, but also to write.

Camp Follower

The press, though, were having their usual dig at Paul. It seemed that they just couldn't get used to the idea that one Beatle could do anything without the others. Paul just ignored all these journalistic put-downs and got down to the job at hand which was doing the thing that he did best: playing and composing music.

By this time Paul the superstar had married Linda Eastman the camp follower, and between them they set about the mammoth task of forming another group to follow in the Beatles' footsteps. Eventually

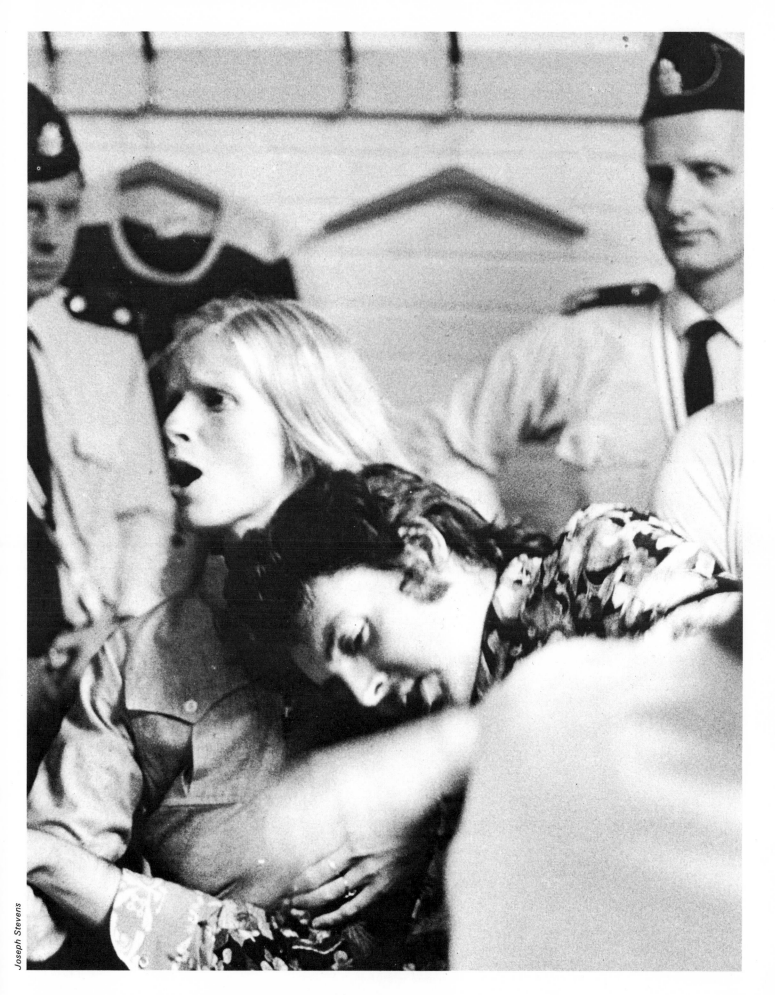

Joseph Stevens

While on tour with Wings, in August 1973, Paul McCartney was arrested by Swedish police in Gothenburg for smuggling marijuana. Above: Linda, protesting on Paul's behalf.

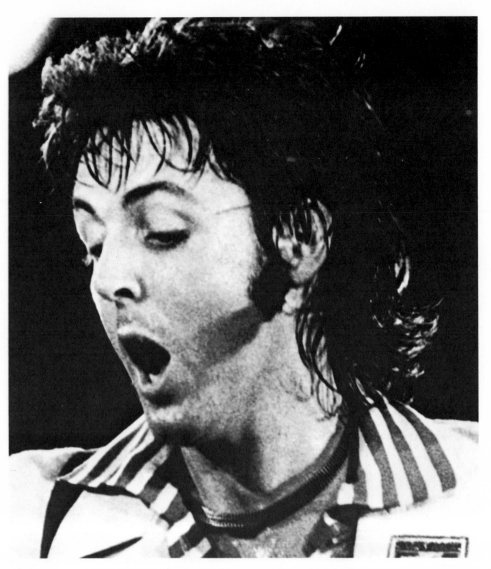

Paul's success continues. His 'family' has found a new audience.

they managed it and, as everyone knows, the new group was called Wings. Henry McCullough had been recruited from the Grease Band, Denny Seiwell from a couple of sessions he had done with the McCartneys in New York, and Denny Laine – an absolute Beatle freak – had been recruited on the telephone. These three, plus Mr and Mrs McCartney, made up the new band. The most incredible thing about Wings is the fact that they have found an audience. No, they're not Beatle leftover audiences either, they are a new breed of pop fans. Many of them have never seen or heard the Beatles, they are prepared to accept Wings for what they play, and the past counts for virtually nothing.

Paul – by now an old pro to the game – decided that he wasn't going to unleash the band on the world (waiting in the wings in anticipation) before he had broken them in.

He did this with a couple of un-announced college gigs and a tour of Europe, visiting such remote places as the South of France, little villages in Germany, and hamlets up in the Swiss alps. Paul, in other words, left absolutely nothing to chance. The press reviews, for all this effort, were no more than lukewarm, but

despite some criticism, the crowds still came out in their masses to see the new band – or at least to see Paul.

Ready In The Wings

After returning from Europe and follow-ing a short holiday, Wings were ready to play to the ever-waiting British audiences. Everyone, it appeared, wanted to see Paul on stage once again. Undoubtedly most people would rather have seen him along-side John, George and Ringo, but they were nonetheless perfectly willing to pay their money to settle for second-best.

It only took one song, 'Big Barn Bed', for Paul's new audiences to realize that they hadn't wasted their money. Paul had lost none of his glittering charisma – he walked on the stage like the return of the Messiah – and the fans went wild. Alright, there *were* four others in the band, but it was Paul they came to watch. It was like the Beatle days all over again. The only difference being there wasn't any screaming – you could actually hear the fullness of his voice, the beauty of his lyrics and the instant charm of his melodies.

Wings' repertoire is based on out and out rock music, with dashes of sentimen-tality thrown in for good measure. Denny Laine, formerly with the Moody Blues, is a better-than-average songwriter whose

contribution to the Wings repertoire is increasing. When Paul moves over to piano, Denny plays bass. When Paul plays lead, Denny plays piano, and when Paul plays bass, Denny plays lead. The two of them complement each other perfectly, and although Linda is always being put down by the press, her harmonies are improving record by record. Perhaps she isn't a marvellous musician, but who needs to be when you have the qualities of Paul and Denny around you. Singles and albums came from Wings at regular intervals, some were mediocre, some were great; but more than anything else, all featured Paul McCartney, and that in a nutshell meant guaranteed sales figures. Sales figures, however, aren't solely dependent on Paul's charisma, his band Wings are very competent. If anything, the musicians within it are more fluent than those of the Beatles.

Search For Musicians

Unfortunately, though, in November, 1973, Denny Seiwell and Henry McCullough left the group after a disagree-ment with Paul. As though nothing had happened, Paul, Linda and Denny Laine went off to Lagos to record 'Band On The Run'. In the end, what Henry and Denny Seiwell had done, so Paul did – as well, if not better. But that was only in the studio. On returning to London it became obvious that the multi-talented McCartney was not going to be able to do all these chores on stage, and so since that moment in time he has been in search of two musicians who will be able to complement his band as well as just play along.

The word superstar is nowadays attached to almost anyone who is lucky enough to get a few singles into the charts. Then, if a successful album should follow, the whole world seems to stand agog. But superstars aren't made from singles or albums, it's all down to charisma. What is it the *Oxford Concise Dictionary* says: 'brilliant or promi-nent person', or 'too exalted for contact and beyond the norm'?

These are the qualities that make a superstar, and a lot of thought should be put into it before someone is so called. Paul McCartney, though, has earned it, and earned it well. From the very early days of the Beatles, Paul was destined to become a star. Maybe he wasn't as super then as he has since become, but all the ingredients were there, it was just a matter of stirring well and then bringing to the boil.

Paul's attitude and secret ingredient to his life and music is simplicity. He is auto-matically the leader of all around him. Show a photograph of the Beatles taken in about 1969–70 to anyone over 35 and then ask them which is their favourite and the answer is more often than not Paul. People follow him like children after the Pied Piper of Hamelin. Paul has shown the music world that simplicity is the mother of invention. In a fickle world, there can't be very many people in pop who have made it twice over *and* retained their strength of personality and the quality of their music.

George Harrison:
The Mystic Maestro

Neither baby-faced beauty nor arrogant sex symbol, George was just the quiet one in the middle . . . playing in the spaces left by two giant egos.

In the touring days of the Beatles, George used to stand half-way between John and Paul and get on with playing his guitar. Then one of them would end the verse and George would stride over to join the other one for the chorus. He'd walk purposefully backwards, playing an economical guitar solo and perhaps throwing in a couple of dance steps. And then he started to write the occasional song for their albums. At first they were run-of-the-mill love songs that the others did better, but then he started turning out strange songs. On first hearing they often sounded normal enough, but . . . whoever started a song with 'If I needed someone to love you're the one that I'd be thinking of'? Soon after this, the Beatles' music became more complex, and as if on cue, out stepped the quiet one to show them the way. George had become interested in Eastern religion, and the next album, 'Revolver', duly marked a watershed in the Beatles' career. 'Revolver' was the only album on which the Beatles ever managed group unity in a serious way, before it they were fun, after it they were each on their own.

George's interest in the East had been a major influence in this shake-up. He was introduced to it by his wife Patti and the two of them went into it seriously. They read and they talked and they meditated, and then they started to spread the word among their friends. Lennon had got really caught up in it, and even Paul's contributions on 'Revolver' had a mystical aura

George Harrison with his wife, ex-actress and model Patti Boyd.

during the filming of *Let It Be* after a huge row with Paul. And although he came back again the problems were not resolved. Basically these centred on George's feeling that he wasn't sufficiently recognised as a writer and musician by Paul. George had just come back from the States, where he had been jamming with many musicians just for the fun of it. The co-operation of these musicians, George said, "contrasted dramatically with the superior attitude which for years Paul had shown towards me musically. In normal circumstances I had not let this attitude bother me and to get a peaceful life I had always let him have his own way, even when this meant that songs which I had composed were not being recorded. When I came back from the States . . . I was in a very happy frame of mind, but I quickly discovered that I was up against the same old Paul . . . In front of the cameras, as we were actually being filmed, Paul started to 'get at' me about the way I was playing."

An Equal Songwriter

This ill-feeling between George and Paul was preserved on the film. At one point Paul says "I always seem to be annoying you." George replies, "All right I'll play whatever you want me to play, or I won't play at all if you don't want me to play." The Beatles' old friend in Hamburg, Astrid Kemp, perhaps put her finger on the background to all this when she observed that George was younger than the others and it took him longer to grow up. Paul had always been something of a father-figure to George and George found it difficult to escape some sort of inferiority complex without over-reacting. Paul, on the other hand, found it difficult to accept that George was by this time his equal as a musician. George was writing as many if not more songs than John and Paul but he wasn't getting an equal share of the cake.

The songs he *was* allowed to record on the Apple albums definitely showed that he was flowering as a songwriter.

His two main themes — love and society — were the usual ones, but what made his contributions different was approaching the subjects from a radically new angle.

The love songs on the Apple albums differ appreciably in feel from any others written at the time. George was not only concerned with the complexity of hang-ups created by Western views of *time* and *change*: loving forever, possessiveness, the inability to communicate. He was also concerned with getting across a simple statement of what he was feeling, of saying, in effect, that if *he* opened himself, then that at least was a start:

'You're asking me, will my love grow?
I don't know, I don't know . . .'

('Something' from 'Abbey Road')

. . . there was no truth in anything else, no need to invoke the past or future to satisfy the present. This notion relates directly to the central reference point of George's Eastern vision: the crucial need

that he never again tried to capture. George's three songs on 'Revolver' marked his emergence as a definite third force, a factor — given the already strained, creative relationship between John and Paul — that was bound to loosen and eventually break up the group.

For a time though, everything went well. Lennon was heavily into acid, George into his enlightenment. For a short time, Paul and George Martin had the group and its talents more or less at their disposal. So arrived 'Sgt. Pepper'. On that album, George had just the one song, 'Within You Without You', which lyrically defined his general position:

'When you've seen beyond yourself
Then you may find, peace of mind,
is waiting there'

Musically, it was George's last attempt at full-scale Indian music. From then on he

began to lyrically explore Western themes through an Eastern-mediated world-view; and in the process create a rock music heavily influenced by Indian moods and tones. 'Within You Without You', had a George Harrison stamp on it, as did John Lennon's contributions. It had become clear that the two of them would not be content to follow Paul's ideas as to the group's direction.

As George's own musical ideas took shape, the last years with the Beatles must have become increasingly frustrating for him; for no matter how friendly members of a group are, there's only so much space on an album. The chance to create tension between songs, to create interacting moods, is something that can't easily be shared. The Beatle albums became less than the sum of their parts; a series of conflicting tracks.

George in fact walked out of the Beatles

BACK TRACK

Born February 25th, 1943.
1966, January: Marries Patti Boyd.
1967, February: George and Patti's first contact with the Maharishi.

1968, February: Studies with the Maharishi in India. November: 'Wonderwall' album.
1969, June: 'Electronic Sounds' album.
1970, September: 'All Things Must Pass' album.
1971, January: 'My Sweet Lord' single. April: Co-writes Ringo's single 'It Don't Come Easy'. July: 'Bangla Desh' single.

August: Organised concert for Bangla Desh in Madison Square Garden, NY.
1972, January: 'Bangla Desh' album.
1973, May: 'Give Me Love' single. June: 'Living In The Material World' album.
1974, November: 27-city tour of the States and Canada, synchronised with release of 'Dark Horse' album and 'Ding Dong' single.

Left: George Harrison was the only Beatle to attend the opening party for Apple Studios. Right: George and sundry other musicians playing at the Bangla Desh concert in Madison Square Garden, New York, in August of '71.

to escape the self. Thus the lament to our society in 'I Me Mine':

'All through the day
I me mine I me mine I me mine
All through the night
I me mine I me mine I me mine'

The sentiments here are spelt out less abstractly in songs like 'Piggies' and 'Savoy Truffle', which remind the listener that George's 'vision' indicates only *two* ways. One way, and 'the sweat will fill your head'; the other way, and 'little darling, the smile's returning to the faces . . . here comes the sun'. Through this period it became apparent that George's voice and his style of guitar-playing perfectly matched his subject-matter. The voice is thin, lacks arrogance, and can float high above the musical ground, forever seeming to reach forward. The guitar-style is similar; long, keening notes hanging in the air — sad rather than painful — above the rhythms flowing beneath.

Shot In The Arm

In May 1970, the Beatles became independent of each other musically and George went solo at a time when the idea-content of rock music clearly needed a positive shot in the arm. The essentially negative business of clearing the ground, dynamiting illusions and generally painting pictures of a world gone mad, had been done in the great creative breakthrough of the mid-'60s. Now, the positive side needed a helping hand — but where was the positive side to be found? The Beatles themselves had always been about enthusiasm and infinite possibilities, all the way from Lennon's sick humour to 'tomorrow never knows'. Now, George in particular seemed to have worked out for himself a way to approach reality through his music that neither contradicted the earlier dreams nor ignored them.

The first evidence of this was the single 'My Sweet Lord', which swept to the top of the charts on both sides of the Atlantic. The album, 'All Things Must Pass', was released a few months later in September 1970. George had spent a lot of time and money on it, using many of the best musicians around and Phil Spector as co-producer. Clapton and Dave Mason helped out on guitar, Bobby Whitlock, Billy Preston and others on keyboards — the list is a long one. The result was a technically flawless record, faultlessly performed. Ultimately though, it would stand or fall on the songs, and, with one exception, these were George's sole responsibility. Those who thought he could only manage two or three good songs a year got a surprise. The 16 on 'All Things Must Pass' were almost uniformly good, melodic and interesting.

This album alone would have been enough to establish George on a level with John and Paul as solo performers, but the underlying philosophic vision took him one step higher, making the album one of the rock masterpieces of the '70s. This vision

is so consistent within itself that it comes almost as a surprise to find it consistent with little else. It's like living in an upside-down room — it doesn't seem strange until you look out of the window. Then suddenly everything in the room acquires a new significance. You begin to wonder how the table doesn't fall off the ceiling, and why

people come through the door backwards with their feet in the air. You begin to wonder what, in fact, is reality.

His love-songs on side 2 of the album, emphasise his strong feelings about the individuality of people and free will, even though the two do merge into one. On 'Run Of The Mill' George states:

*'No one around you will carry the blame
      for you
No one around you will love you today
      and throw it all away'*

. . . for ultimately

*'Only you'll arrive at your own made end
With no one but yourself to be offended
It's you that decides . . .'*

Not that George himself is that strong. In 'Let It Down' he worries all the time about other people's opinions of him. But he knows his feelings and recognises his weaknesses, hoping that sharing them will eliminate them to a degree. Compassion is at the heart of his songs.

Love between two people is also part of something wider to George, part of the way of approaching living here in the material world. The rest of 'All Things Must Pass' illustrates both this wider vision and the control George has over all the components of his music. The basic philosophic vision underpins it all, expressed not as philosophy but as a series of 'moods' occasionally illuminated by flashes of lyrical insight.

To have found strength in the truth that nothing is certain and that nothing survives, a truth that is central to all Eastern ways and so foreign to the West, is a measure of the distance George has travelled spiritually. That he can convincingly communicate that strength in the rock idiom, is a mark of the distance he has travelled as a musician.

Occasionally, on 'All Things Must Pass', the underlying Hindu world-view breaks surface, almost as a preface to his second album, 'Living In The Material World'. 'The Art Of Dying', for instance, deals with re-incarnation in words that make little allowance for Western sensibilities.

'Do you believe me?', George sings hopefully. The final track, 'Hear Me Lord' is a straight-ahead prayer, not a multi-religious pop anthem like 'My Sweet Lord', but an act of devotion, of total commitment:

*'Help me Lord please to rise a little
      higher
Help me Lord please to burn out this
      desire'*

In a society bombarded with sexual aspirations, that plea is likely to find few sympathetic ears. As a song though, 'Hear Me Lord' succeeds because it conveys in the music a mood far wider than the lyrics suggest. The old Harrison-Spector formula of the relentless flow cascading down to flow yet again, has never been done better.

Then, in the summer of 1973, came another carefully structured album. 'Living In The Material World' had taken two and a half years to make, and this time offered a specifically Hindu view of the world. Once again though, the music transcends the particular. It charts George's journey of self-discovery, starting with the simple invocation: 'give me love, give me peace on earth'. From there George works his way through illuminations and limitations, Beatle hassles and drug hassles, to a calm

George harmonising with Bob Dylan at the Bangla Desh concert. Their song 'I'd Have You Anytime' was later released.

acceptance of what he thinks life in the material world must be all about.

Musically, the album sounds like a river, from the tumbling stream of 'Give Me Love' through free-flow and rolling majesty and down to the oceanic serenity of 'That Is All'. The music and the vision once again fit each other perfectly. At the time of its release, in fact, many critics were prompted to suggest that George had at last made a real connection between rock music and social commitment.

George has always been stereotyped as the Beatle who was most concerned with money, but an early anecdote of the Cavern days tends to undermine this. A girl waiting outside didn't have the money to get in. George slipped a few shillings to the Cavern bouncer, saying ''give'er this and don't tell'er I gave it to yer''.

In the later days of success he has given away money to what he thinks worthy causes, less perhaps than Lennon but with rather more care and with less publicity.

But the most obvious thing has been his organisation of the Concert for Bangla Desh, which began with a visit from his old friend Ravi Shankar —

*'My friend came to me with sadness
      in his eyes
Said he wanted help before his
      country died'*

For the concert George coaxed both Eric Clapton and Bob Dylan out of their semi-retirement. The music itself was an amazing success, but the concert was much more than that. It was described in a music paper as 'a brief incandescent revival of all that was best about the '60s . . . the magnificence of the music and the selflessness of the motives were proof that the art and the spirit are still alive.'

Apart from 'Living In The Material World' nothing much was heard from George after the Bangla Desh concert until the announcement of a major US tour in the late autumn of 1974. Together with Ravi Shankar and an 18-piece orchestra of Indian musicians, Billy Preston and a rock group of supersessionmen including Willie Weeks on bass and Tom Scott from Joni Mitchell's backing-group the L.A. Express, George took the States by storm. Visiting 27 cities with 50 concerts, George was again in the forefront of rock.

Somehow, though, despite the tour, a successful album released to coincide with it, an acting role in a film of the play *Little Malcolm And His Struggle With The Eunuchs*, and his production role on albums by Ravi Shankar and Splinter, George remains, as always, 'the quiet one in the middle'.

Ringo Starr: Mr Versatility

As John Lennon once affirmed in an interview, ''The Beatles would *probably not* have been as successful without Ringo.'' To think that anyone could have asked such a question, and especially at a time when the standard Beatles answer to any interviewer's question was to be found somewhere in among a flood of Liverpudlian wisecracks and private jokes, itself testifies to the low profile that Ringo maintained during those heady years of the '60s.

Nevertheless, while there were always conflicting reports about the identity of the *fifth* Beatle — Brian Epstein, George Martin and Pete Best all rated — it was always well understood that Ringo was well-and-truly a Beatle.

Ringo's story is well-known. While John, Paul, George and Pete Best sweated through their apprenticeship in Hamburg and Liverpool, Ringo learned his trade around the coasts of Britain working in summer holiday camps. He didn't play on the first single, 'Love Me Do', or on any of the early demo tapes. When the cover photograph for 'Please Please Me' was taken, he still hadn't got his hair straightened out, Beatle-style. Yet, after a childhood of persistent illness, the tide turned for him and he signed on the dotted line at the exact moment of Beatle take-off.

Many people have claimed, cynically, that Ringo was the luckiest person of the decade, and certainly he received more than his share of malevolent criticism; but all that ignores the very real contribution that he was able to make to the success of the Fab Four.

Ringo may indeed have been — as *A Hard Day's Night* suggested — the fall guy, but equally he was always able to command the loyalty and deep affection of the others. (Indeed, he has since become the first Beatle to engage the services of all the others for a solo album.) Equally, while it was left to the others to chart new musical directions, Ringo always seemed to move comfortably in their wake, content every now and again to bash out old C&W numbers like Buck Owens' 'Act Naturally' or

L.F.I.

Ringo turned furniture designer with one of his steel creations.

Carl Perkins' 'Matchbox' and 'Honey, Don't'.

Ringo was the first to settle down to a happy family life, and where John eventually married a Japanese-American avantgarde culture-freak, George a top British model, and Paul an American photographer, Ringo opted for a hairdresser from Liverpool — Maureen — whom he'd known from the early days and has stayed with ever since — still holding her hand. He quickly got down to the business of raising a family — Zak was born in 1965 and Jason in 1967 — and affirmed his intention of opening a chain of hairdressing shops. In other words, Ringo has never pretended to be anything other than a home-lovin', lawabidin' man. He is the only one of the four never to have been convicted of drug offences; and when the Beatles were all performing their spiritual exercises with the Maharishi in Wales, Ringo, down-to-earth as ever, said it all reminded him of the holiday camps . . . and came home early.

The Sweetest Of Them All

Ringo, said Hunter Davies in his official biography of the Beatles, was 'the sweetest of them all really', and that's probably his raison d'être: Ringo, the nice guy. It's both unnecessary and facile to observe that the Beatles couldn't have been the force they were without each member taking a distinct part that fitted perfectly into the whole. Therefore, Ringo's contribution to the group was as essential as anyone else's.

Even having said all this, the fact remains that most people thought when the four Beatles went their separate ways, Ringo would be the one who would first sink to the bottom. In the years since, however, Ringo has remained as much in the public eye as ever.

On the surface, Ringo never had too much going for him. He, after all, was the one who played drums. "He's very touchy about his drums," George had said in *A Hard Day's Night*, "they loom large in his legend." His playing though was never particularly outstanding: he could never do a roll, and in the beginning was restricted to occasional elaborations on thump-thump-bang-thump. But he persisted, and showed continuous improvement — his playing on the 'White Album' and 'Abbey Road' is particularly good — in the process developing a recognizable style.

Of his vocal abilities, there's not much to say, save that he's certainly no Caruso. His voice is a flat, pleasant monotone for which John and Paul used to write special songs. The first was 'I Wanna Be Your Man', from 'With The Beatles', though on the first album he had delivered 'Boys', an old Shirelles' number, with characteristic enthusiasm. The songs that were subsequently written for him, 'Yellow Submarine' for example, always seemed to emphasize the affection which the others felt for him. 'With A Little Help From My Friends' may have been composed with deliberate irony, but anyway it was the quintessential Ringo song. John and Paul had got Ringo down to a 'T' — he had such a winning, affable personality, and so many friends, that his own failings were irrelevant, since he never needed to do anything on his own.

In the Beatles' feature films too, it was lovable Ringo who was singled out for special treatment; he was the thinker, the loner. In *A Hard Day's Night* (the title of which he had thought of) he was the butt of everyone's jokes, the one who was mocked and treated unfairly. He was rewarded with a scene to himself, walking dolefully along the bank of the Thames. It was a scene which provided the film with some of its more wistful moments, and won Ringo much critical acclaim. Afterwards, though, he claimed that he had been drunk at the time, and that the success of the scene was a fluke. Then, in *Help!*, he was Ringo with one enormous ring too many, and that was the core of the plot, such as it was. ''Why do you wear so many rings on your fingers?'' he was once asked. ''Because I can't get them all through my nose,'' he retorted.

Finally, it should be mentioned that the complete works of Ringo Starr, up to the dissolution of the group, amounted to just two songs — 'Don't Pass Me By', from the 'White Album', and 'Octupus's Garden' on 'Abbey Road' — and even then a scene from *Let It Be* showed George helping him to write it.

When the time eventually came for them all to stand or fall on their individual reputations, Ringo quickly surprised everyone. For a start, he already had two solo film roles behind him (a bit-part in *Candy*, and an outstanding leading role in *The Magic Christian*), and when the Beatle break-up became inevitable, he was quickly out of his starting-blocks with two solo albums by September 1970.

Pub Songs

Both of these albums were special projects that came into the 'things-to-get-off your-chest' category. The first one, 'Sentimental Journey' was something of a joke, and failed on every conceivable level except the all-important one of providing Ringo himself with some satisfaction. It was an album of standards that Ringo remembered hearing heartily sung in his local pubs back home in Liverpool when he was a kid. A sentimental journey, right; also, one would have thought, a rather private one, and many people still believe he should have left it on his own tapes at home.

Ringo nevertheless entered the project whole-heartedly, and, characteristically, had no trouble in persuading various first-class reputations to come along and produce one track each. It's difficult to imagine, for instance, that Quincy Jones, Johnny Dankworth and Elmer Bernstein would have done the favour for anyone else. The idea of having a different producer for each track (Paul McCartney, for example, directed 'Star Dust' in a super-schmaltzy manner) was to acquire a different 'fee!' to each number — but this was

never satisfactorily achieved. The major problem was that Ringo's voice and swing standards like 'Night And Day' and 'Love Is A Many Splendoured Thing' were never meant to come within a hundred miles of each other. 'Bye Bye Blackbird' was really the only song that worked well, and that's jokey anyway.

It Came Easy

The second album, later that same year, was a different matter entirely. Ringo had always liked C&W music, as his choice of songs from early Beatle days had indicated. This time, however, he was invited by steel-guitarist Pete Drake to record a complete album in Nashville, and was granted the services of the cream of local studio musicians — from Jerry Reed right through to the Jordanaires. Since Pete Drake had also obligingly commissioned all the songs from top country writers, this was one time it did come easy for Ringo.

The album was engineered by Elvis' old guitarist, Scotty Moore, and the company was in fact so distinguished and talented that Ringo didn't even have to play drums — what everyone had always thought he did. In the end it was Ringo's album only in so far as he sang the lead vocals on it; but who else could have assembled such an army of respected talents?

Ringo's contributions left the spirit of Nashville intact, and the album was accurately titled 'Beaucoups Of Blues' (he pronounced it 'boo-coos'), and contained many maudlin songs of love and death which Ringo delivered in his usual carefree manner:

> '. . . Found her with another man
> In a fit of anger he took her life and the
> stranger's
> Then he took his own
> Um . . . love don't last long'

Still, Ringo sounded quite cheerful about it all; even so, there's a natural dolefulness about him — 'If I talked about the good times/there wouldn't be much to say'. It's perhaps as well Ringo doesn't get taken that seriously.

Needless to say, the production made use of every trick in the book. 'Beaucoups Of Blues' might easily have been a classic C&W album had the vocals been of a different ilk, but then that was never the point . . . was it?

'It Don't Come Easy' was an archetypal Ringo record, and his first single. It was written by himself and George Harrison, who produced it in a sort of sub-Spector fashion; but it was a belting, driving song that was perfect for Ringo's voice. The lyrics were plain and typical — 'got to sing the blues, if you wanna sing the blues/ but you know it don't come easy'. In the States, it provided Ringo with his first Gold Disc, whereas 'Back Off Boogaloo', his only other real single, was not quite as powerful and not quite as successful.

With these projects out of the way, and

SKR

Ringo Starr, the slicked-back greaser in his rocker gear, and wife Maureen. He is no longer instantly recognizable as the wholesome, cuddly Beatle he once was.

BACK TRACK

1968: October, had a cameo part in *Candy.*

1970: April, *The Magic Christian* opens in London – Ringo in star part. 'Sentimental Journey' released. June, flies to Nashville to record 'Beaucoups Of Blues'. September, 'Beaucoups Of Blues' released. December, Paul files suit for dissolution of Beatles.

1971: February, Ringo said in High Court that McCartney acting like a 'spoilt child'. April, 'It Don't Come Easy'

released (reached no. 5 in Britain; no. 1 in US). July, filming *Blindman* on location in Spain, and also writing the score (which never materialised). August 1st, appears at Madison Square Garden with George Harrison *et al* in Concert for Bangla Desh. December, *200 Motels* opens with Ringo in lead role.

1972: January, 'Bangla Desh' LP package released. March, 'Back Off Boogaloo' released (reaches no. 2 in Britain; no. 10 in US). T. Rex concert at Empire Pool, London, which Ringo filmed for *Born To Boogie*. August, filming *Son Of Dracula* with Nilsson.

October, *Born To Boogie* opens in London. *That'll Be The Day* goes into production, shooting on the Isle of Wight. December, agrees to take part of Uncle Ernie in Lou Reizner's *Tommy* production at London Rainbow, but pulls out and is heard only on the album.

1973: April, *That'll Be The Day* opens. November, 'Photograph' released (reaches no. 8 in Britain, no. 1 in US). December, 'Ringo' released. *Blindman* opens in London.

1974: January, 'You're Sixteen' released in US – reaches no. 1. November, 'Goodbye Vienna' album released.

Top pic.: Ringo Starr, as Mike, in a scene from *That'll Be The Day*, the film that portrays the '50s beautifully. Below, L.H. pic.: Harry Nilsson played the Son Of Dracula in the film of the same name. Ringo, plus beard and whiskers played Merlin the Magician. Above: Maureen and Ringo and friends. Main pic.: Ringo as a Mexican bandit in the film, *Blindman*.

with the exception of his appearance at the Bangla Desh concert at Madison Square Garden, Ringo otherwise diverted his attention from making what he off-handedly describes as 'pieces of plastic'. Each of the Beatles had had individual film work before Ringo, but ultimately it was he who was more attracted to the cinema.

In *Candy* he had portrayed a lecherous Mexican gardener, and in *The Magic Christian* – also taken from an original work by Terry Southern – he played the unruly nephew of Peter Sellers. If he wasn't entirely successful, it wasn't so much his fault as the film's, since his part had been invented for him as there was no such character in the original novel. He wasn't then a great actor, but he did provide occasional moments of humour, and was emphatically not the embarrassment that many unkind people had suggested he would be.

Blindman was a bloody Western, made on location in Spain, in which Ringo played a passable Mexican bandit. Even so, it appeared an ill-judged attempt by Ringo to broaden his acting experience by playing a dramatic role in a film that took over two years to open in Britain, and was instantly forgettable at a time when violent, neo-Peckinpah Westerns were two-a-penny.

His next film was *200 Motels*, written and conceived by Frank Zappa, in which Ringo played the part of Frank Zappa(!). The film was made by Tony Palmer, although long before it opened he had publically dissociated himself from it. While embodying a certain anarchic quality, the film was nevertheless moderately disastrous. Made in the post-*Tommy* era, when rock stars liked to think themselves masters of several art forms, *200 Motels* was one of the events that proved conclusively that few of them were.

Crazy Ideas

During 1972 Ringo himself took up directing. However crazy the idea might have sounded, he was in a position to indulge his craziness, and anyway the Beatles had already made their own film – *Magical Mystery Tour* – although that had given them their first-ever taste of artistic failure. Ringo had several projects in mind, but only two he carried to fruition. The first one was a documentary about Marc Bolan, who was then at the zenith of his career, called *Born To Boogie*. Much of the film surrounded a T. Rex concert at London's Empire Pool in April, 1972. If it proved anything it was perhaps that Ringo could occasionally point a camera in the right direction, and that Marc Bolan was considerably out of his depth as 'superstar' material, as he didn't have the character to carry a whole film – something which the Beatles themselves had once done so successfully.

The other film, *Son Of Dracula*, starring Harry Nilsson – another of Ringo's show-biz friends – had a soundtrack by an ad-hoc grouping of Ringo, Nilsson, Klaus Voorman, Peter Frampton and John Bonham, but for some reason its release just didn't follow. Then, towards the end of 1972, Ringo eagerly accepted the opportunity to play the part of a philosophizing Teddy Boy in a film designed to catch the vogue for '50s nostalgia, *That'll Be The Day*.

The film was, as expected, an enormous success, and Ringo played his part superbly. All he had to do was act naturally, and – whether working on a fairground, as a holiday camp barmaid, or wising-up inexperienced David Essex to the best way to lay girls – he was entirely at home in the part, infusing it with his own irresistible sense of humour. Ringo was brilliant – easily the most authentic thing in the film, which collapsed two-thirds of the way through when he was written out.

Helping Out

That'll Be The Day was given a general release in Easter 1973, and in December Ringo crowned a personally successful year by releasing his first solo rock album which, as though to emphasize that, was called simply 'Ringo'. Once again, even if Ringo *isn't* a reincarnation of the Great Caruso, his voice – if not melodic – has a warm and friendly quality that is perfectly suited to many of the songs on 'Ringo'. Once again many eminent rock musicians turned up to help out, and the production – by Richard Perry – was quite magnificent. With a fine collection of material, the album is one of the most rewarding of the Beatle solo ventures, though its release was at the time overshadowed by Paul's 'Band On The Run'.

What was especially triumphant about 'Ringo' was that here Ringo had established a precedent for the eventual reunion of the Beatles. All the others had written songs for the album; John's song, 'I'm The Greatest', displayed a welcome return to his tongue-in-cheek humour, and 'Six O'Clock' was one of the most appealing tunes that even McCartney has ever written. The Harrison-Starkey composition, 'Photograph', released as a single, hinted at that old, romantic flavour:

> *'Every time I see your face it reminds me of the place we used to go.*
> *But all I've got is a photograph and I feel like you're not gonna be back anymore'*

It did well in America, and his next release, 'You're Sixteen', provided him with yet another no. 1.

If the Beatles were ever to get back together again, Ringo may well have been a prime agent in the business. Even so he has admirably proved his ability to come from the Beatle shadows and achieve things for himself. In his spare time, he's even been busy designing furniture.

The three songs that best define Ringo are 'It Don't Come Easy', 'Act Naturally' and 'With A Little Help From My Friends'. So it hasn't been easy, but in films he's acted naturally, and in music he's got by, as few others ever could, with a little help from his friends.

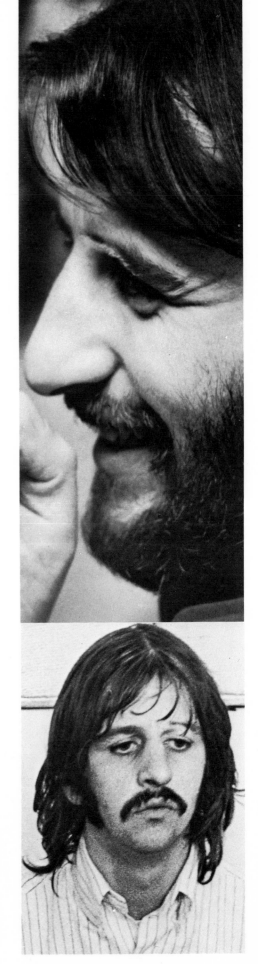

Above: two moods of Ringo.